# DIFFICULT
# PEOPLE

# DIFFICULT PEOPLE

## A Gateway to Enlightenment

LISETTE LARKINS

RAINBOW RIDGE
BOOKS

Cover and interior design by Frame25 Productions
Cover photograph © djgis c/o Shutterstock.com

Published by:
Rainbow Ridge Books, LLC
140 Rainbow Ridge Road
Faber, Virginia 22938
434-361-1723

If you are unable to order this book from your local
bookseller, you may order directly from the distributor.

Square One Publishers, Inc.
115 Herricks Road
Garden City Park, NY 11040
Phone: (516) 535-2010
Fax: (516) 535-2014
Toll-free: 877-900-BOOK


Visit the author at:
www.lisettelarkins.com

Library of Congress Cataloging-in-Publication
Data available upon request.

ISBN 978-0-9844955-6-8

10 9 8 7 6 5 4 3 2 1

Printed on acid-free recycled paper in the United States of America

This book is lovingly dedicated to
Jeannette and her family,
who, somewhere along the way, became my family

# Contents

# Foreword

LITTLE DID I REALIZE in July 2008, when I employed Lisette Larkins as my personal assistant, the many and incredible ways she would prove invaluable to my wife and my family and eventually change my way of thinking, or I should say, living. At that time, my wife, Jeannette, who had been diagnosed a few years earlier with early-onset dementia, or Alzheimer's disease (they are essentially indistinguishable), still insisted on driving her own car, despite my concerns and the concerns of her physicians and family. Although her cognitive facilities were impaired, she was still functional; i.e., she was able to dress and feed herself, converse, and play golf. She had trouble, however, paying bills and remembering appointments and kept asking repetitive questions—the signs of early dementia. So, Lisette's primary functions at first were to monitor the check paying, reconcile the check register, return phone calls, and arrange appointments for me and my wife; essentially to keep track of these household duties that my wife previously had been responsible for doing.

Within months, Jeannette's disease took its course, and we had to take away the keys to the car, which created no end of destruction and distress for all concerned. Gradually, her functionality became further impaired, and Jeannette needed assistance with cooking, eating, getting dressed, and other routine tasks. Eventually Jeannette totally lost her ability to speak and swallow, leading to the need for a feeding tube and assistance in just about everything else.

I soon became concerned for Lisette's own well-being, and the possibility of "burn out," resulting either in her own potential health problems or her need to "flee" a difficult environment. I tried to alleviate the constant pressures of her dealing with Jeannette's deteriorating condition. For example, I offered to employ another assistant to help her and encouraged Lisette to take days off to "recharge her batteries." But she insisted that she was fine and that it was important to her to continue to deal with the situation on her own, without additional professional caregivers to relieve her and further complicate Jeannette's life.

As difficult as it was to believe, Lisette genuinely seemed to be realistic when she would repeatedly respond with "no problem" to my every concern for her well-being. Even the most violent behavior by Jeannette; e.g., her temper tantrums and refusal to be fed through the G-tube, appeared to be "no problem" for Lisette. I started to question whether Lisette was really normal or was truly a "super person" of some sort. I kept thinking of the old saying, "If it appears too good to be true, it probably is." How could I ever replace her if she were to leave?

What I didn't realize until I reviewed the draft of Lisette's book was exactly how she was able to turn a nightmare for any caregiver—dealing not only with long hours and an afflicted person's severe impairments and distress, but the agonizing emotions and worry of her whole family—into "no problem." As things worsened with Jeannette, due to her increasing impairment and need for 24/7 assistance, it seemed that Lisette got even calmer and was better able to respond to not only Jeannette's needs, but also the emotional well-being of other members of the family.

When I started reading her manuscript, *Difficult People: A Gateway to Enlightenment,* it was as though a mental storm had come to an end: the clouds started clearing, the wind and rain stopped, and the sun started to shine through. I then realized how Lisette was able to perform at this high level, fulfilling not only the ever-increasing needs of Jeannette, but at the same time managing our residence and other properties and staying on top of other household duties, all the while quieting Jeannette's distress and discomfort.

Until I personally witnessed how Lisette was at peace and always happy, it would be an understatement to say that I would have been skeptical of concepts like "chronic well-being." Had I not had the opportunity to observe her in action every day, I would not have even engaged in any discussion about "enlightenment," let alone agree to read a book about it.

As a trial lawyer for many years, my professional life has focused on hard, concrete facts, persuading others that the facts and legal arguments I make are more credible than those argued by my adversaries. In almost every legal matter, as well as some personal matters, I approached things with an adversarial attitude. I believed that whoever said "winning isn't everything" must have been a loser. There was no second-place finisher in my life: just winners, and losers. I did not have the time or inclination to search my head or soul very often, or even contemplate the possibility that there could be a different approach to what I was thinking or who I was.

In my world, not counting my family, there was only one person—me. I never thought about whether my mind was different from "me" or whether some part of my mind actually sought out and engaged with other competing minds. Reading Lisette's description of pathways to more enlightened living, and how to achieve a quieter and less chaotic and "noisy" mind, became fascinating and challenging. It is now clear to me how she is able to do all that she has done with Jeannette—and done it so well and peacefully.

It is obvious that Lisette has truly mastered what she describes, and frankly she has changed how I look at and now respond to difficult people and situations. Because I am a practicing lawyer and my thought processes are grounded on evidence and logic, I face problems and challenges, meeting them "head-on." After reading what Lisette writes about so convincingly, and observing how effectively she uses her practice in real life, I'm convinced that many of the ideas are both credible and practical. Her description of nonreactivity may not be readily acceptable to everyone or may not seem achievable. But I certainly see it work for Lisette, and it is working for me now.

As of this writing, Lisette is still Jeannette's full-time caregiver and manager of the household. As a result, Jeannette and I are very different and much better today, thanks to Lisette's enlightened way of living life. Lisette is convincing proof that what she writes about really works.

*Jeannette's husband*
*February 10, 2011, Malibu, California*

# 1

# The New Ashram and Guru: Everyday Problems and the Difficult Person

LIKE MANY SPIRITUAL SEEKERS, I yearned to know the truth about myself as an immortal being; to experience what it was like to have the mind's compulsive thinking actually stop. Only an enlightened person could experience such chronic bliss, blessed with a predictably graceful ability to embrace whatever showed up as the present moment. Such masters resist nothing. They are gentle, peaceful beings.

To know ultimate freedom from reacting emotionally to the ups and downs of life with its inherent periodic mental suffering, to attain self-realization in the same way that other spiritual masters have, is the ultimate attainment for any serious seeker of spiritual truth. Such an experience of self-realization occurs as a gradual process or in a burst of awakening for the student who is ripe, spiritually speaking. Attainment of self-realization is the prize to which every spiritual sage has aspired since the beginning of time.

Like many seekers, I assumed that realizing this permanent

state of well-being, in which stillness of mind prevails, was an achievement possible somewhere in a distant future. Meanwhile, like every other person I knew, my noisy mind rattled compulsively. There were many moments of peace daily, but such inner peace was not unshakeable.

Then, in 2005, an inner prompting urged me to leave my position in Virginia as sales director for Hampton Roads Publishing Company; to leave a long-term romantic relationship; to leave behind my identity as an author of three books about the deeply spiritual nature of extraterrestrial contact phenomena, which included a role as speaker and radio guest.

Moving from the East coast, back to the home of my childhood in Southern California, I had no idea why an inner force was calling me or what my next step would be.

Returning to Malibu, I lived with my divorced mother. My father soon joined us, in need of care for his terminal cancer. My grown siblings were there too, one who recently had had a baby. Nephews and nieces came to stay or visited often. As a woman in her late forties, I found this curious indeed: to find myself again living with my family of origin. At one point my grown son even moved to the Malibu property.

With ages ranging from ninety-one to newborn, the environment was ripe for spiritual practice because there were so many differing cherished viewpoints floating about. Any individual who was able to peacefully coexist within such a loaded and diverse environment and remain unshakably and demonstrably accepting and content would be remarkable.

It was not that there were lots of arguments, but rather, as a long-term student of the practice of stilling the noisy mind, I noticed that mine still had lots of secret thoughts of judgment or correction. Although I was aware that this was the normal state of most everyone's mind—chronic comparing, contrasting, and judgment and its attendant self-righteous feeling of being offended—I wanted a more heightened spiritual perspective for myself.

Due to the nature of my lifelong extraterrestrial encounter experiences, which are the subjects of my books, I was already somewhat of a so-called spiritual teacher in the realm of opening to a spiritual life. Because of these experiences, a spiritual opening had already happened for me, and I tended to look deeply at life's meaning, shunning trivialities and meaninglessness more than the average person. Perhaps I was already able to observe my own deficits with courage.

This introspective nature developed naturally as a result of living outside of the norm of human existence with respect to ET-contact phenomena. When you are having extraordinarily unusual experiences that the culture says are impossible, it's predictable that such a catalyst will trend the experiencer toward either of two directions: embrace more fully your own spiritual growth by actually practicing what you're learning, or succumb to mental suffering and develop psychological problems. Contactees from all corners of the globe write me for guidance, having been shaken themselves by bizarre paranormal phenomena. They want to share their own experience of sudden spiritual awakening that occurs as a result of often transcendent, deeply spiritual experiences.

But now back home amidst relatives, the words of spiritual teacher Ram Dass rang true: "If you think you're so enlightened, go spend a week with your parents." Clearly, my spiritual practice needed tweaking. It felt suddenly hypocritical to advise anyone of anything. And I had no idea how I was going to earn a living.

As I considered my new living arrangement, I decided to approach my spiritual seeking with renewed earnestness. A fresh willingness to uncover a deeper state of being arose, and an even stronger call to awaken fuelled my resolve. Redoubling my efforts at spiritual growth, I attended more workshops, enrolled in more training, read more spiritual books, and in general tried to fix myself more fervently.

But three years passed with no appreciable spiritual gains—or no letup on the internal turmoil. I had gotten a good job and was now earning over six-figures annually as a manager of a busy Beverly Hills four-surgeon medical practice. I did my best to apply spiritual concepts to working life, but the hectic pace usually split my attention. A new romantic relationship began. My website forwarded emails to me from readers that went unanswered until I finally closed it down. Considering that perhaps I was making no spiritual progress lately, and with the imminent end to that new romance, I wondered if perhaps enlightenment was impossible after all.

There were plenty of reasons to believe that a full awakening was unrealistic in these modern times. How many ordinary seekers had actually attained enlightenment? With the exception of a lucky few who had done so spontaneously when on the brink of suicide, or following isolation with a guru in India, it seemed that no ordinary, relatively well-functioning seeker had won the spiritual lottery while working nine-to-five.

What seeker, I reasoned, sought enlightenment by refusing foreign spiritual travel tours or sitting at the feet of a traditional ashram-based guru? Who had stayed on the job, returning home nightly to demands of kids and family, juggling the bills, and had still achieved enlightenment? Surely, we mainstream seekers were sliding backwards down the spiritual path, stubbornly clutching our lottery ticket of hope for that elusive peace. If enlightenment or an enlightened way of living is possible, then it should be possible as a householder. The promise of spiritual attainment can't be such that it eludes 99 percent of the people outside ashrams or demands that a person be a trust-fund baby able to live in meditative seclusion without needing auto insurance or having to relate daily to worldly oriented family and friends. And yet the inner call still sounded. It would not go away. The hope for enlightenment or an elevated state of being still burned inside from visions years earlier during which a spiritual master appeared, encouraging participation in my own awakening. The clarion call of this vision was unmistakable: Enlightenment is possible for anyone who earnestly desires it.

Despite doubts, but with the vision's hopeful promise urging me on, I again read my copy of *The Power of Now: A Guide to Spiritual Enlightenment,* by world-renowned spiritual teacher Eckhart Tolle. Applying Tolle's teachings again, this time I did so with renewed courage and discipline.

For good measure, I considered that maybe a personal guru was needed, someone I could study under on a daily or weekly basis. Praying for the right spiritual teacher to show up in the flesh, I was now prepared to make whatever change was necessary or to move anywhere or do anything if it would tip the karmic scales in my favor. Awaiting a signal from heaven above, I updated my résumé and resigned from the medical practice. The job didn't feel right, nor did writing more books at this time or speaking publicly. Although there were a few more radio interviews to do that had been previously scheduled, I vowed to conduct those and then drop out entirely from my life as an author. What my next move should be, I could not yet say.

Now able to utilize several months of unemployed quiet in which to pore over Tolle's books and CDs, every morning I gathered his material in the shade under a palm tree for the day's study. Every few hours I'd take a juice break in the house and email another résumé for a job that I didn't really want. Letters from readers still arrived, having been forwarded from my publisher. Guiltily, I added them to a large box of other letters and replaced the lid.

Open to receiving spiritual guidance in whatever form it came, I was now prepared to relocate to an isolated ashram. If a new workshop would do it, bring it on. Even though Tolle's teachings cautioned that the inner journey to self-realization was a vertical one deeper into self, requiring no horizontal travel, I wasn't totally convinced. Surely, something complex or expensive needed to be added as an adjunct to effective spiritual practice. Praying for a real teacher, a true teacher, a *final* teacher, to present himself, I patiently awaited whatever was required to enlighten me.

Soon after, what proved to be the exact and perfect vehicle for my awakening presented itself in the form of my next job—caring for a woman in the middle stages of Alzheimer's disease. When the position was first offered to me, my mind had many objections: the pay wasn't right, being a caregiver seemed too menial, and the family wanted to start me on a part-time basis only. But despite my mind's resistance, a quiet, inner urging asked me to step into the unknown.

A general medical dictionary defines Alzheimer's disease as a progressive neurologic disease of the brain that leads to the irreversible loss of neurons and to dementia. The clinical hallmarks of Alzheimer's are progressive impairment in memory, judgment, decision-making, orientation to physical surroundings, and language.

However challenging the mental and physical symptoms may be for the patient—and the sympathy one feels for their suffering—to the student of spirituality, observing the mental processes caused by dementia and the attendant resistance to those changes by her and her family, became the catalyst that fueled my awakening.

It was not that observation of the disease itself caused any particular insight. Instead, what was instructive was observation of the chronic *objections and resistance* to the challenges of the disease, as expressed by the patient and by her family and friends. This resistance was observed to be a perfect microcosm of the resistance of, and hence mechanics of, suffering that we all experience through normal daily living. By virtue of my opportunity to closely observe the inherent dysfunction in the way every mind objects to what *is*, the conclusion that presented itself was stunning albeit unpopular in its implication: all mental suffering was self-induced, no matter the so-called reason for that mental suffering.

Physical suffering as a result of pain and illness, in addition to any kind of mental suffering from loss, can act as a catalyst for a spiritual opening as the sufferer seeks a deeper meaning of life; however, this is not the case for everyone. Some people grow more hardened, effectively shunning a golden opportunity to soften the hard shell of resistance. This softening is the soil where the seed of spiritual growth can finally take root. If no softening occurs, the sufferer continues to seek meaning through shallow means, such as hanging on to self-image and seeking approval of others through appearance, actions, or accumulation.

Although physically and mentally healthy individuals are not offered this golden opportunity to suddenly awaken spiritually, physical or mental suffering is not *needed* for spiritual attainment. All that's required is to become astutely aware of the dysfunctional mechanics of mental suffering—so-called normal human mental processes—which is at first easier to observe in others, and then to observe the same mechanics alive in yourself.

The purpose of this book is to help you to more fully participate in this new paradigm for realizing enlightenment by helping you in three areas:

1. You will be provided an effective context and process for a perspective shift regarding *who* your final teacher really is. In

other words, the guru who can *ensure* that you attain enlightenment comes in the form of your everyday problems, and particularly any difficult person in your environment. This difficult
person—hereafter referred to as your "DP"—is someone you
may have mistakenly believed is *blocking* your spiritual progress
by shattering your peace of mind.

2. During this process you will be able to uncover what is
really blocking your full essence from being revealed so that self-
realization can occur. This means that what normally troubled
you about a DP in your immediate environment can now act as
a *catalyst* for spiritual awakening. Rather than becoming upset,
and emotionally reacting to the DP, you now can recognize their
dysfunction and remain blissfully unmoved despite their often
extremely negative dysfunctional patterns.

3. While reading this book, you may recognize that *you* are a
DP. This is a blessed recognition and is so beneficial that the date of
this realization might even replace your annual birthday celebration
as a date of significance. Since every DP suffers intensely, and also
creates untold suffering for those in their environment, recognizing your status as a DP will finally help you dissolve this complex.
Only someone whose cognition is impaired, e.g., an Alzheimer's
or dementia patient, may be unable to implement strategies to
consciously reduce mental suffering in themselves and others.
Everyone else is a potential spiritual master ready to awaken.

Common, yet dysfunctional, mental processes block spiritual
growth. To be able to observe the nuances of these dysfunctional
mental processes alive within you creates immediate relief. When
you apply an effective spiritual solution to remedy those dysfunctional processes, your self-realization arises. But first it is helpful
to observe the mechanics of dysfunction in another so that you
can then recognize your own inner DP. As such, being in the
presence of any DP fills this need perfectly.

Whether you observe the behavior of a difficult coworker, spouse or ex-spouse, family member, alcoholic, lover, mother-in-law, person with a mental illness, or patient suffering from a mental disease such as Alzheimer's, the precise relationship between the observed and observer is immaterial. If *you* are a DP, as we all are to some degree, the solution is applied in the same exact manner. All that is required is that you become willing to "use" another's difficult personality by observing it without judgment. When patterns of dysfunctional mental activity are seen for what they are, you are on your way to healing your own dysfunction. You simply recognize the nature of the beast and apply the antidote for immediate relief.

The antidote, despite the mind's insistence that it is arduous and lengthy, is actually quite straightforward. There is nothing at all mysterious about transformation in consciousness. Mental suffering is caused by our mind's chronic objecting to and fault-finding with people, circumstances, events, and oneself. In order to establish internal peace, one uncovers the peace that is already there but is obscured by this chatter. The process of uncovering this peace involves gradually becoming more *aware* of the peace and stillness that is already there by focusing on the present moment, then one naturally becomes more and more aligned with it on a permanent basis.

This is the process that I used to successfully uncover all my own insane mental processes, thus I was able to awaken fully. By "using" the DP, I mean to say that the difficult personality or the misguided mental, physical, and emotional reactions that produce difficult personalities, can serve as an invitation to heal ourselves. Ultimately, by observing a DP in my own environment, an invitation presented itself to let go of dysfunctional assumptions that we all take for granted.

This is why it was so helpful to have been offered a position as caregiver to a woman who was in the throes of such extreme mental suffering, and as it turned out, helpful for her as well. Although I had no training whatsoever in the field of professional caregiving, I assured the family that I was up to the job as Jeannette's caregiver. Soon, I was caring for her full time at their private residence.

During that three-year period, Tolle's simple but effective spiritual practice of staying in the present moment was adopted by me with the understanding that it was my only hope in surviving the demands of Alzheimer's. The anger and denial that permeated Jeannette's existence was very strong. As can be imagined, her negative emotions were extreme reactions to losing her memory, her mental clarity, and her physical health and abilities. These are the precise identifications that we all take for granted as being a normal way of looking at ourselves. We identify with the beauty and agility of our youth; we identify with our accomplishments and abilities. We erroneously believe that we *are* those roles, forms, or attributes. Hence, we suffer when we witness deteriorations of the body, image, health, wealth, and relationships. And yet, we will all experience these losses at one time or another, as much as we wail against that fate.

If ever there was an opportunity to witness the nuts and bolts of the pitfalls of "resisting what *is*," my role as caregiver to a woman with Alzheimer's disease was the premier opportunity to create an ashram out of my working environment. Whatever so-called problems arose within this environment—in keeping with the stated goal of any ashram—Jeannette's home became my training camp for enlightenment. Her problems and her difficult behavior, rather than being tolerated or avoided by me, were recognized as the quintessential opportunity for spiritual growth and greater compassion for her suffering and ours.

Observing Jeannette's denial and strong resistance to her

disease became my profound new spiritual practice. It was nothing short of flabbergasting to recognize that her reactions to her disease mirrored our own reactions to the provocations of daily living. Although we may not have dementia, there were unmistakable corollaries between her daily angry confrontations, denial, and resistance with one type of loss after another, and our own confrontations, denial, and resistance as we meet the challenges and losses inherent in everyday life and in response to all types of DPs. Ultimately, the difficult person's behavior doesn't matter except as it shows you its inner reflection.

Although the diligent spiritual practice that I applied caused instantaneous inner peace no matter the degree of Jeannette's chronic resistance, it also uncovered a surprising and profound ability to appreciate whatever circumstances arose. By noticing my own resistance, the truth became evident: there is no problem at all; there is only resistance to something that the mind *says* is a problem. Strong identification with thinking and pseudo roles soon dissolved in me. In other words, I stopped believing that my thoughts were necessarily true. Like most people, I had assumed that what my mind believed was gospel.

A chronic state of well-being soon emerged. This is the state of enlightenment, or one definition of it, and is available to each of us. This unshakeable inner peace makes the "normal" way of living with its chronic resistance and the mind's good and bad labeling seem almost incomprehensible in comparison. Finally, this bliss, so documented in ancient spiritual texts, was immediately understood as the only meaningful human goal.

This awakening was juxtaposed against Jeannette's ever progressing Alzheimer's, a disease infamous for its attack on one's identity, abilities, and relationships, and the rage and confusion that develops as a result. Despite most people's immediate agreement that her situation was catastrophic, my own deepening insights produced full acceptance of what *is*. A deep understanding was revealed of the futility of mental resistance. It was shocking to fully recognize that the source of Jeannette's acute mental suffering, and the suffering of her family and friends as they witnessed her deterioration, at its deepest level was not due to Alzheimer's per se, but was due to the *resistance* to the reality of Alzheimer's' effects.

Changes in abilities, possessions, and status in a healthy mind do not have to automatically produce suffering. This means that it's only the *resistance* to loss and change that creates suffering. And since every single one of us is aging and moving closer to our own death, I soon recognized that her journey was merely an accelerated version of each of our own, whether or not we are aware of it. The contrast between my deepening peace produced by my diligent spiritual practice, and the intensifying mental resistance and suffering by those in my midst, was ironic at the least.

After awakening, it was quite surprising to witness the way in which most everyone seems to have forgotten that each of us is on the road to aging and, ultimately, dying. Each of us will experience physical and mental decline and loss of status and material possessions. As we age, we lose status and dignity, youth and beauty, and mental and physical agility. Alzheimer's, although seemingly affecting only those with the diagnosis and their families, readily presented itself as the symbolic, albeit condensed, challenge of everyone. Jeannette became my symbolized and "perfect" DP. Our navigation of ordinary life as I helped her with daily activities became a microcosm of everyday problems that almost everybody complains about.

As we age, not one of us will escape the necessity to become aware of the ways in which we each argue with what *is*. This resistance puts us in chronic opposition to the present moment. The present moment always offers stillness and peace, yet most people chronically try to fill it up with noise. When we avoid the peace inherent in the present moment, we instead focus on what's wrong. When we do this, we say that we are upset because we have "a lot of problems to deal with." This is Alzheimer's personified: responding to life's events with an angry and defiant "No!" to what has presented itself.

Becoming consciously aware of the slow but certain eventual loss of cherished mental identities, physical health and abilities, and attachments to possessions, the stages of Alzheimer's might as well have been prescribed for any advanced student of spirituality as a graduate course. As any serious spiritual seeker can attest, the ideal spiritual practice demands that the student align with present circumstances and let go of the chronic need to be in control of that which cannot be controlled.

The advanced spiritual student learns to remain peaceful and unmoved despite surrounding chaos. To be chronically reactive, chronically in judgment of and condemning of present circumstances and others, the patient with Alzheimer's demonstrates what is wrong with us all. Suddenly, my new job as caregiver was an opportunity for me to view the way that I, too, had lost sanity. Recognizing that in normal culture, it's considered perfectly normal to argue incessantly with life's ups and downs, Alzheimer's effects were suddenly evident in every single person I observed, including myself.

Hence, the perfect ashram had sprung forth, complete with a guru, Jeannette. Her demonstration of the dysfunction of refusing to accept what must ultimately be accepted beautifully mirrored to me where my own work needed to be done. Jeannette's disease of Alzheimer's showed me how it operated within me too. Whatever roller coaster of emotions, vehement judgments and objections, or moods and anger were expressed, I came to recognize that her disease was alive in each of us, varying only by degree.

Jeannette's disease was my disease. Alzheimer's disease's almost absolute intolerance of the present moment allowed me to see where I too rebuked life. By loving her despite her combativeness, I began to love everyone. In observing her deficits without judgment, I was able to fully observe my own deficits without judging myself.

Jeannette was not always difficult. There were many times when, suddenly, out of her mental confusion arose an opening, and the love that she expressed to me and others was sweet and pure. At these times her true essence shone through. Suddenly there she was, at peace, very still, only her hand moving silently as she drew with crayons in her Disney coloring book. Such moments highlighted how each of us, despite character deficits, has a lovely essence always hiding there, even if obscured by false identifications and extreme mental noise and its incumbent suffering.

As a state of enlightenment within me began to reveal itself, it was not a surprise. During this time, I recognized that resistance to other people and their moods or to my outer circumstances was futile, and I let go completely. "Presence," that still yet powerful life force that is ever-present as described by Eckhart Tolle, then permeated me and became my natural state of being.

As my perfect spiritual teacher, Jeannette embodied the universal condition. Her embattled mind, only by slight exaggeration, was every man and woman's obstacle to peace: a compulsively noisy and chronically resistant mind structure that takes the person over and pretends to be them.

The spiritual dilemma to be overcome had painfully, clearly, unmistakably made itself known. Dissolve that part of the negative mind that is present in everyone, whether or not an Alzheimer's or dementia diagnosis is present, and you could transform your every experience.

But simply observing your own DP's dysfunctional mind

is not enough for spiritual growth. You must notice the same, although perhaps lesser, patterns of noisy resistance in your own mind. Without using an awareness of *another's* mental chaos to magnify recognition of your *own* mental chaos, no significant spiritual gains are possible.

As Jeannette presented to me the bane of human existence—the never-satisfied-for-long mental condition that believes that by objecting to what *is*, somehow that will change it—something was shifting in both of us. As her disease progressed, I could feel her letting go of the sadness of her condition. In her own way, she was preparing to die, and an opening was created where the light shone through. Also, as Tolle has noted, the rising of Presence in a person affects everyone in contact with them, and it could be that my own awakening, to include the love and support of her family and friends, was having a beneficial effect on Jeannette.

In her agony—especially during such times—she embodied the Great Teaching because by sharp contrast, the way *out* of suffering became so apparent to anyone who cared enough to notice: only a still, quiet mind offered relief from any kind of problem. Only by accepting the present moment as it is would anyone stand a chance for realizing a chronic state of well-being. And so, I consciously joined the journey with her in all its stages and heartache. She became my spiritual practice, and by close observation of the mechanics of her mental struggle, it became a catalyst for my growth.

This book is being written over the course of eight weeks, post-enlightenment, and came so easily and naturally that it virtually wrote itself, much like a player piano plays without need of an operator. Often, notes were scribbled at stoplights as I chauffeured Jeannette to doctor appointments or ceramic classes, while observing the precise dynamics between us that I impart in these pages.

Jeannette's behavior regularly illicits creative impulses in me to write what I'm observing. At this very writing, I am sitting at the kitchen table with her while she fiddles with her rings and earrings and sorts them into sandwich baggies. This book is being written entirely during my live-in tenure in the last months or years of her late-stage disease.

Sometimes I awake naturally at 3:00 A.M. and write for a few hours prior to her waking up at 6:30 A.M. when I deliver her breakfast through a tube in her abdomen. These tubal feedings often produce a fury of wailing and fingernail scratches as she protests the syringes that contain her liquid meal. When Jeannette's G-tube was first placed, feedings occurred every two hours, so there was ample opportunity to observe the mind and its palette of negative reactions. With all this drama, it's no wonder I was able to awaken, spiritually, during this time. My choices were either to consciously awaken spiritually or to collapse under the stress in the environment, as do many caregivers of DPs.

There is profound awareness that without the challenge of Jeannette's chronic resistance to just about everything, including the combativeness so characteristic of the disease, motivation for relief would not have produced such disciplined adherence to my spiritual practice. But do not make the mistake of assuming that the practice is difficult.

The only difficulty is really just the initial discomfort in tweaking your perception of reality: ultimately, your spiritual growth can be hastened by the degree of your participation and the recognition that the process of awakening can indeed actually arise within so-called ordinary life circumstances. When we rightly conceive of problems and difficult people as potential catalysts for growth, we are finally on the fast track in participating personally in the flowering of human consciousness.

Of course there are many challenges. We must awaken within a culture and daily environment which generally condemns, rather than accepts, the circumstances that arise in any given present moment, which rejects the importance and transformative opportunities borne from stillness. Most people revel in a noisy environment, needing to constantly fill up the room with actual noise or mental noise by a focus on minutia. The spiritual seeker embraces that which a normal person complains about. The advanced student of spirituality recognizes the profound possibility to open spiritually within the context of meeting the challenge itself by simply making friends with the present moment, no matter what that is.

Accepting the present moment does not mean that you must stand still while someone clunks you on the head. Peaceful presence does not mean allowing abuse or becoming inactive or subservient within a professional context. Making friends with the present moment is a qualitative shift in accepting what is already in place. Then, once accepted, changes can be initiated, but from a peaceful clarity that a noisy mind can never match in effectiveness.

Awakening can happen through a disciplined approach to uncovering presence. Presence is the life force, that pure, animating no-thing that brings life to form. Presence is already there, but is obscured by mental noise from a focus on meaningless minutia. Ultimately, there is no greater contribution to a family, neighborhood, or country than to be a peaceful bringer of more presence. This peaceful countenance creates no further harm, and in fact, creates a ripple effect of well-being. Awakening is not only possible, but is every human's responsibility and is already happening within each person, whether or not they are aware of it. Awakening, spiritually, is the movement toward healing, in which identification with compulsive negative thought begins to lessen, and identification with the essence of life broadens and expands. Inherent in the awakening process is a corollary decrease in mental suffering.

This book is about how I integrated the spiritual teaching of Eckhart Tolle and applied it to my ordinary life as caregiver to a woman with Alzheimer's disease. Although this tenure produced this book, my role in caring for Jeannette naturally expanded and developed into that of a "spiritual caregiver," which was its primary function. My purpose is to encourage and inspire you to cease delaying the awakening process, no matter your age, occupation, living situation, or degree of spiritual awareness.

Freedom from the enslavement of the mind and the manner in which it produces compulsive thought and chronic resistance to the present moment is the great shift that is now possible and is actually occurring around the world. Every facet of life benefits from human beings who grace their environment with a peaceful countenance. Finally, the essence of life is uncovered, and true creativity and purpose can be freely expressed through you. Without chronic mental noise and resistance, those who live or work with DPs, and even DPs themselves, are freed permanently from the nightmare of mental suffering and chronic complaining and faultfinding.

Like a thick gray fog dissolving over an aqua blue sea, your true essence can finally emerge. This is the mythological Promised Land wherein a state of being arises that needs nothing to feel complete. Whoever most resists the present moment causes the most suffering for themselves and others. This is why awakening spiritually is so important.

A state of chronic well-being and a deep peace that will never leave you are truly possible. But your participation is required. Effective spiritual practice, as described in the following chapters—and when applied with diligence—will bring spiritual transformation.

The peaceful state of being that once seemed almost impossible to achieve now becomes the new "normal." Life becomes simple and sweet. All problems and DPs are cherished and seen for what they are: a moment in the now that requires nothing except your gentle "Yes."

Difficult people are not limited to those in your family or work environment. DPs are everywhere. They are the rude waiter, your ex-husband, the abrupt flight attendant, your troublesome brother-in-law, or your child's schoolteacher. Whoever bothers you, by word or deed, is *your* DP. In addition, whatever behavior of yours that bothers you can be now identified as that of your own inner DP. Every day, almost without exception, yet another person's behavior, language, action, or style will be considered abrasive by you. Sometime, sooner or later, you will become irritated by someone who is "getting under your skin." When you find yourself disapproving of someone—or even yourself—meet your new guru. A stellar opportunity in which to grow spiritually has finally presented itself. This recognition is the moment for which your soul has long been waiting.

Once resistance to problems and DPs dissolves, ironically, every area of your life actually improves. This is the ultimate spiritual paradox and the demonstration that the Source of Life really does have a sense of humor after all.

# 2

## Using the Difficult Person (DP) and Any Problem as a Mirror

IN THE THREE YEARS since I became Jeannette's caregiver, her condition has progressively worsened due to Alzheimer's disease. Where there was once a beautiful and vital woman whose strong golf swing could hold its own against the men, she rapidly declined into a late-stage condition in which she had trouble swallowing food and liquid, and eventually her own saliva. At this point, her friends and family could barely contain their sorrow at seeing her. A strong and competent woman originally diagnosed as "early onset" at the age of fifty-eight, she exhibited by sixty-eight many of the mental, emotional, and physical characteristics of a much older woman.

Throughout her life, Jeannette had been adept at commanding and managing the circumstances of her environment. Her husband tells the story of when the two of them owned a successful restaurant on the beach in Malibu. He said that while they were in the middle of eating dinner themselves one night, she noticed a nearby table that she felt had not been promptly cleared by the busboy. Despite her husband's protests and to the surprise of other guests at neighboring tables, who did not know that she was the owner, Jeannette jumped up herself, stacked up a pile of dirty dishes and lugged them into the kitchen.

At my initial job interview, after Jeannette's impairment began to affect her ability to manage their household, it was evident that Jeannette's position had been thwarted as her husband overturned her objections and sought out an assistant. When I arrived, she stood at the far side of the room glaring at me with her arms folded in front of her. When her husband coaxed her over to introduce us, she nodded curtly but refused to say anything. I knew that if I had extended my hand to shake hers, it would have been rebuffed. It took quite a long time for her to warm up to me, but even then, any hint that she was being helped, coaxed, or controlled elicited a strong reaction. Once, upon exiting a public restroom together, I noticed that she had accidentally left her purse in the stall, and I returned to get it for her. As I held it out to her, she snatched it from me angrily, furious that I had tried to steal it from her. This scenario was constantly repeated with her purse, a jacket, or any other personal items that she would set down and forget almost every single day for three years.

Most significant were the emotional reactions of friends and relatives as they witnessed Jeannette's decline. After all, this was a woman with a quick wit and fast tongue, one who when faced with a problem or challenge was confident she could solve it. Once, as a student pilot on a solo flight from Los Angeles to Bakersfield, she pulled the throttle out too far and it came out in her hand. Receiving detailed emergency instructions from the control tower, she fixed the mechanical problem while still flying her Cessna at 2,000 feet and was able to land the plane safely.

It was common to hear reactions from friends such as, "My heart breaks to see her this way." Or, "I feel so sorry for her." Observing the way and manner of her mental confusion, physical deterioration, and chronic resistance was distressing to everyone who encountered her. I could also see in their sincere response a little of the dread we all feel about our own eventual incapacity. Last night, after proudly holding up her coloring book to show her husband a dancing girl with pom poms, he took her by the hand to the wall near the pantry where many enlarged photographs of her were displayed. He wanted to show her that, she too, had once been a dancer like the girl in the coloring book. Pointing to a picture of Jeannette, then in her early twenties, super-model gorgeous, a dancer who once attended Julliard, he said, "Look Jeannette, you did this too. You used to be a dancer." But she did not recognize that the young model with long honey-colored hair was indeed her. As her husband dabbed a tissue to her mouth to catch a little drool, he sadly shook his head.

Although I, too, experienced moments of grief due to witnessing the sudden transformation of my beloved charge, particularly *after* my awakening, I could not lose sight of how Jeannette's mental state matched everybody's own "condition." Classic Alzheimer's symptoms are more apparent as a symbol of the dysfunctional, albeit normal, mind than is the average DP's because the lows are so extreme. All of us have encountered, at some time or another, DPs who create frequent havoc with those around them.

As a child, I remember my father, who, when he returned home to six children, tired and frustrated after a long day at the office, became easily agitated and overreactive, a true difficult person. One evening, as my beloved cat approached his leg purring, my father kicked the cat, and somehow the cat got caught on the top part of his foot and went sailing up to the ceiling. As a seven year old, it was a strange feeling watching my lovely kitty being hurled through the air by my father. Like any child, I recognized how much negative influence and power an angry person can exert over others, and I wanted to stay out of his way. Without benefit of any effective solution, DPs can shape the emotional tone of their surroundings, often exerting tremendous manipulation in families and relationships by using their anger as a weapon. In addition, for reasons that will be explained in the next chapter, DPs actually *need* drama and conflict, and thus, to the detriment of those in their environments, chronically seek out the most minor incident and blow it up to unconsciously prove that problems abound.

Sustained peace is virtually impossible in a DP's household or common work area. Sometimes, their negative characteristics may seem to be only slightly exaggerated to that of the non-DP, which of course is the point entirely. These characteristics include:

- The sudden and surprising rise to unprovoked anger;

- Cherished opinions that are held as absolute;

- The chronic attempt to hold tightly to past memories and to tirelessly seek satisfaction in past accomplishments, or the hope of finding satisfaction in future accomplishments or activities;

- The need to have constant attention on items of accumulation as a means to forestall boredom or to gain a sense of importance;

- The utter inability to remain still and quiet without need of mental busyness and meaningless distractions or focus on minutia;

- The unquestioned trust in conceiving of exercise, nutrition, or dietary preferences as the premier means of gaining and sustaining physical and mental wellness;

- The inability to recognize that the quality and accessibility of inner serenity, rather than the quality of muscle tone, physical agility, appearance, body weight, or financial portfolio, are the sole means to the greatest of all accomplishments: peace and lasting well-being;

- The inability to recognize strong identifications with roles, forms (things of matter), and attributes and to place them in their proper perspective as temporary, fleeting, and subject to change.

From my observations as caregiver to Jeannette, seldom did others notice the way in which Jeannette's Alzheimer's characteristics were manifested in them, for the simple reason that most everyone is operating from the same dysfunctional playbook. It is only when such seemingly normal characteristics become somewhat more exaggerated in the dementia patient, is one considered to be "affected by the disease."

Topping the list of unwanted Alzheimer's characteristics is the fact that it's a terminal diagnosis with no cure as of yet. But then, even if a cure were to be found, that too is only temporary. Eventually death arrives packaged in some other cause, and if it's sudden without a slow loss of faculties, this then makes us happy? Oddly, it is usually the patient's death that often seems to cause the strongest outcry, as if we've all been hypnotized and pretend that everyone is not subject to *some* form of death, at some time or another. It's as though as a culture, we have all met while on vacation at a resort hotel, and we become hysterical and sad because all the guests will leave at different times. That's what happens with bodies. We all eventually leave.

So really, even while Jeannette's deteriorating physical condition would probably outpace others', it would just be by a few years or a decade or so. As anyone can attest who has aged to their forties or fifties, a decade goes by in the twinkling of an eye. So why are we bemoaning losing someone to a similar if less exaggerated process that is coming up for us in the *same* twinkling of an eye? It's puzzling how so few friends and family are able to accept that Jeannette's chronic mental resistance to her slow movement toward death is an inescapable reality currently alive in them too.

To verbally point out how each of us is subject to the same impermanence is considered to be insensitive at best and cruel at its worst. But is it? It would be saner if we love deeply during the time we have together; then, when one of us leaves the "hotel" of life, we accept it, recognizing our transient nature, rather than denying it.

A healthy perspective recognizes that the arrival and departure of travelers is the natural rhythm of life. The tendency to deny your own impending dissolution, or the dissolution of a loved-one, is deeply ingrained and will not easily soften, unless and until you contemplate the fleeting nature or impermanence of all things of form. This is a saner and ultimately more humane way of handling our own and others' physical decline, rather than emulating the terminal patients' harsh reactions to their impending death. We are all slowly dying. How can we live more fully right now? The answer is to find a way to cease the mechanics and patterns of mental chaos and its suffering in ourselves, which ultimately then reduces the suffering that we impose on others.

However, there are built-in perceptual blinders when it comes to observing and correcting neuroses in oneself. It's much easier to notice and react to outside problems and DPs. Indeed, few of us are able to objectively observe our own most misguided character deficits because such patterns stay hidden in the shadows of our awareness, no matter how much pain those deficits cause us. Of course, we don't usually characterize classic Alzheimer's symptoms, or the normal resistant response to difficulties, as deficits when observed in the patient or anyone else for that matter. We nod in understanding that the disease has taken the patient over, and so it has. With respect to Alzheimer's patients, mental flaws are not considered to be character flaws, but rather that "terrible debilitating illness." With everybody else, mental flaws in which offense is taken by one thing after another is considered to be evidence of a *life* that has problems, rather than evidence of a *whacky mind* that has problems.

So what do we do about the undiagnosed "normies" who exhibit virtually the exact same characteristics as the dementia patient, although maybe to a slightly lesser degree? For starters, we can admit that like them we too are chronic whiners, in which we habitually object to life circumstances, like a spoiled adolescent whose rich daddy won't buy him a country.

There are plenty of people who habitually display difficult behavior and cause chronic suffering to themselves, their family, and friends and who have no diagnosis whatsoever, short of being a DP. We can agree that Alzheimer's symptoms are dysfunctional when embodied by the patient in mid- to late-stage, but when those same defects are present in healthy people, we call it "normal."

Most people would refute this suggestion, countering that with Alzheimer's, it's the *degree and frequency* of mood changes, temper tantrums, the hoarding of possessions, chronic and predictable relationship fluctuations, and clinging to past memories and fearing an unknown future that separates their diagnosis from normal human behavior. However, what is really happening is that, culturally, we have "normalized" our own and others' dysfunction. We have simply succumbed to tolerance of a low standard of quality of life. Many people believe that they are already introspective and can readily admit to flaws that require improvement; however, we are not speaking here about *unusual* flaws. We are addressing normal mental activity that we all consider appropriate, but is actually bitterly misguided and loaded with suffering.

It is only when the serious spiritual seeker becomes interested in *mastery* that the highest levels of functioning becomes possible. When mastery is present, suffering is absent; and a chronic sense of peace and well-being take up residence, no matter your physical state or outward circumstances. It is within this context of serenity that all areas of life become enhanced. The beauty of awakening spiritually is that this state of chronic well-being is permanent, no matter the physical or mental circumstances that surround you. Who doesn't want that?

A sense of pervasive well-being is not possible without a corollary decrease in your own noisy mind with its chronic focus on minutia. Most people don't recognize that a noisy mind is characterized by moodiness or chronic judgment of others or circumstances. When the noisy mind is finally stilled, perhaps for the first time in a lifetime, there is a marked decrease of crabbing about the present moment. The journey to uncovering this quiet mind and ensuing lasting peace that this state generates is what this book presents. We will explore the busy state of the normal mind as experienced by almost everyone, juxtaposed by a discussion of what life begins to feel like when the noisy mind is quieted.

As strange as it sounds, one does not need a healthy body, a good memory, access to material objects, intellectual finesse, or (gasp) even longevity to be at peace. How unusual indeed to consider that a person who knows how to still their chaotic mind is functioning at an altogether higher order of living than a difficult person, who by definition is chronically moaning that something is not right (again!). Whereas the more common DP among us, meaning each of us, relentlessly pursues exercise, diet, professional and financial goals, and educational pursuits as a means for happiness and well-being, there's enough evidence of successful, beautiful people who are miserable to conclude that there is something missing from this scenario.

If you replace the focus on the body's shape, muscle tone, and appearance as a goal to well-being with the focus on the human *mind's* degree of quietude, true, lasting, and unshakeable peace is realized. Then you can work out in the gym with carefree abandon, rather than undertaking exercise with clenched-fist determination in forestalling death. Rarely, if ever, does the exerciser question the condition of their chronic and compulsive mind and the need to work out the kinks in *it*. Of course, there is nothing wrong with exercise. The emphasis here is on pointing out that without the benefit of a quiet mind, no amount of exercise can equal the benefits gained by a person whose compulsive thinking has been stilled. Mental stillness, not exercise or material gain, is the only guarantee of a peaceful life.

Further, if we drop the assumption that the cause of suffering is from loss of mental or physical ability through age or disease, loss of dignity and possessions, or loss or change in relationships—in an Alzheimer's patient, DP, or healthy individuals— we are finally unraveling the great lie. *Only* resistance *to what is can create suffering.* When you are able to become aware of the true present, to fully accept what *is,* immediate peace is uncovered. You may not feel happy, or have happy feet—that temporary state achieved after gaining something of material value or gaining an ego boost. But, with respect to a hierarchy of states of being, peace beats out happiness as a more stable and deeply experienced state. To be graced with a permanent sense of peace is indeed the highest and most deeply satisfying existence.

Unhappiness, or suffering to any degree, has become a normalized state of being when we think we don't have what we want; however, few of us can tolerate the truth behind the *actual* cause of any kind of suffering. Certainly, in the care of the Alzheimer's patient, virtually no one dares to confront the way that the disease mirrors everyone's challenge that must be faced sooner or later: chronic and compulsive resistance to the impermanence of form—resisting what *is*.

This is truly the only real "problem" after all. Of course, there appear to be myriad difficulties that need our attention, or require a decision. Hardly anyone argues the fact that things seem to go wrong constantly. But do they really? What if the only thing that goes "wrong" is the suffering that we experience when we cannot accept what *is?* Ultimately, this is the only real "problem." Resistance to what appears in the present moment *is itself* the "problem." This is solved by the only possible solution: acceptance of the present moment as it is. Action or correction comes second. But first one must accept with a calm and quiet mind whatever *is* occurring. Out of this quiet state, right timing is correctly recognized and right action is thus borne.

No human being will escape the challenges of aging and the inherent challenges that we all face as we exist in a complex world; however, it is only our strong and immature demand that events, circumstances, and people must stay static and not change that causes our anguish. When we resist what *is,* we suffer. But we almost never recognize this as the cause of our suffering. We hardly ever dare to recognize just what is the core issue.

When the Alzheimer's patient is prescribed mood-stabilizing

medication, there is an unspoken assumption and agreement that the patient's erratic moods are a natural human reaction to their decreasing abilities and level of functioning. It is assumed that the patient has every right to be upset. Rarely, if ever, do physicians, family, or friends offer the sufferer a broader context in the face of their suffering. In other words, most people can relate to others who are complaining. They have no other context in which to view such complaining, whether other's or their own. There's always a good reason to complain that we ourselves can understand all too well; we agree that life is difficult. So when we hear someone complain of their problems, we silently are grateful that their problems are not our own.

Instead, once you wake up from the cultural delusion that maintains that mental suffering is part of life, you cease agreeing that crabbing is a normal healthy outlet necessary for emotional catharsis. Instead, the degree and frequency of your complaints and chronic focus on meaningless minutia loudly declares your degree, or lack of, spiritual maturity. It is far from healthy to complain, and to humorously explain away such a chronically negative state as that of being "fiery," is another way of denying just how toxic a habit complaining to ourselves and others is.

During one of Jeannette's frequent appointments with her physician, I was asked to report on the state of her agitation. After describing how Jeannette reacted angrily when I tried to feed her via the G-tube, the doctor responded, "Of course she's upset by such frequent feedings. Reduce them to three times per day." Then, at our next check-up, I was again asked about Jeannette's aggression, at which time I reported that she continued to physically and emotionally object, despite the fact that the frequency had been reduced. "Of course she's upset," the doctor said, "she has a G-tube." In the almost three years since I have been her full-time caregiver, rarely, if ever, have I heard a friend, family member, or treating physician gently but firmly respond to Jeannette's anger with a verbal refuting of the actual cause of her mental suffering. In other words, there is a definite general cultural consensus that does not recognize the true but actual cause of mental upset, namely, in Jeannette's case, that it's not the G-tube that is causing any of her mental suffering, but her abject refusal to conceive of the G-tube in any other way than that of a problem. The analytical mind complains, chronically. Of course, the analytical mind is upset. It exists for only this reason and so it relishes our concession when we "acknowledge" its pain, that it's upset or angry, because it deeply yearns for us to notice its suffering when we "acknowledge" its pain.

If you happen to live with a DP, you may agree that to respond to another's fury in a calm way while remaining internally peaceful is a wonderful goal, but not that easy to practice. I fully understand and remember how, after many months of trying to gain Jeannette's trust of me as her caregiver, she had finally softened and actually began to look forward to our outings together. On one such afternoon, two years before I was fully able through effective spiritual practice to remain in a state of unmovable peace despite her negative reactions, we pulled into the driveway of her home. She had anticipated that her three olive trees in the front yard, which had been scheduled to be trimmed, would have been completed. Instead, the trees remained with full branches, no tree trimming had occurred.

At the sight of them, Jeannette flew into a rage and began slamming her fist on the car window and dashboard. She yelled out in anger, cursing and furious that the tree trimmer had not even begun his work. Internally, I cringed, gaping at her in disbelief. Unable to control my reaction, I blurted out, "It's just a tree trimming for god's sake!" At my response, she bolted out of the car, slammed the car door with the force of a bulldozer, and stormed into the house. She then refused to acknowledge me for the next few days, and it took many days to regain my lost ground.

The emphasis here is not that it's important or necessary to get a DP's approval; the emphasis is on putting into place an effective spiritual practice that virtually guarantees that you can remain thoroughly peaceful despite whatever raging and chaos occurs in your environment. When you gain chronic internal serenity, all mental suffering disappears. Finally, one's true power is realized because no one or nothing can move you from your peace.

In the example of Jeannette's reaction to the untrimmed olive trees, of course, as I reacted to her reaction, I was demonstrating the exact same negative behavior that she was: she whined about what she was beholding, and then I did the same thing, as I beheld her reaction. Jeannette's overreaction is just an exaggeration of our own resistance when confronted with radical change, loss, or even simply objecting to outcomes or circumstances that don't meet with our approval, no matter how benign. Even in this case, our friends and family support our dysfunctional negative reactions by agreeing that yes, of course we should feel terrible about losing our mates or our jobs, or our invented insistence that life should be as we demand that it be. It's considered to be a normal human reaction to respond negatively to changes that we don't want.

Each of us stays ignorant to our own, albeit less severe, dementia and how it manifests in us when we yell at what *is*. When we do so, we stay stuck in the nightmare that has us believing that dying is the opposite of living and therefore, we are doomed and deserve to be miserable in our reaction to the knowledge. Or, to quote Dylan Thomas:

> *Do not go gentle into that good night,*
> *Old age should burn and rage at close of day;*
> *Rage, rage against the dying of the light.*

In actual fact, life has no opposite. Although death is the opposite of birth, "life force" is synonymous with your ever-present "inner essence" that can never be destroyed. It is constant and never changing. Your inner essence is synonymous with consciousness, or "presence." Both of which point to the same loveable purity of being that underlies every personality. It is the same precious, invisible quality that animates the adorable puppy. It is the ever-present force behind everything.

The challenge arises because most of us are asleep in the cultural nightmare in which we grieve the fluctuating nature of that which must fluctuate. All forms, by their nature, continually arise and then dissolve. This changing nature of form is evident in all of the blessed cycles on Earth and includes weather patterns, pale yellow roses, and human bodies.

Form can never, ever stay static. Matter can never stay the same for long. Bodies cannot stay static. Most humans are in a constant state of resistance and denial to this one bare and incontrovertible fact. Change is happening within every single structure of matter, whether a human body, apartment building, cactus, or bumblebee. All that is born or made grows or expands, and then declines and eventually dissolves. Mental resistance is simply pretending that change is not already happening everywhere. And mental resistance is made manifest through myriad examples of the compulsively noisy mind.

Most of us are not aware to any degree of the way and manner in which our *own* minds are noisy. The solution to this blind spot is to "use" the demonstration of *others'* anger, bad temper, moodiness, impatience, PMS, etc., as a mirror. When I started working with Jeannette, there were times when I was stunned by instances of her mean impatience, chronic faultfinding, and tireless focus on meaningless minutia. Of course, she also exhibited a dynamic, caring, and fun-loving personality, but it did not last very long until it was usurped again by her complaining. From her perspective, no doubt, my very presence in her house was a constant reminder of her declining abilities, and so naturally she may have saved her worst behaviors for me, within the privacy of her own home; however, after the incident in her driveway in which I overreacted to her overreaction, I went home that night and cried myself to sleep. After only a few weeks, I realized just how hard this job was going to be. Perhaps there was a reason that three or four other caregivers had come and gone before me. The job was hard. Jeannette, it seemed to me, could be mean-spirited, and almost embarrassingly arrogant in her lack of gratitude for all the areas of her life that were astoundingly abundant—at least from a material perspective. As I lay there in bed, I wondered why I was judging her when I couldn't control my own reaction, and yet I was unafflicted. Suddenly I realized that Jeannette and I were doing the exact same thing, reacting to the curves the river of life threw us. Suddenly, I saw that I was hardly any different from her. It was that evening that I resolved to never again fail to notice how my own negative reaction to anything wasn't any different from hers. And because over the years that ensued, I would witness such distasteful behavior on her part, I, as promised, noticed how in some way, all such reactive behaviors were alive in me too.

This is the context in which I undertook the deepening spiritual practice that is described in this book. There were deep and profound realizations that were more potent than normal because of the intensity of my environment. As a student of spirituality, my conundrum both invigorated and challenged me. The challenge had been presented: grow spiritually or suffer right along with Jeannette. I decided that the only sane response was to attempt to reduce both our suffering simultaneously. In that one decision, my life became transformed, and I can only pray that Jeannette's life, too, was positively affected.

The key then, as a simple beginning, is to start to notice others' resistance, chronic complaining, and chronic focus on meaningless minutia, then notice your own as it presents in a similar or even dissimilar manner. It's hard to look at our own flawed personalities directly, so first see it in another and then notice it in yourself.

When we are able to see our own patterns in others in our immediate vicinity, whether at home, work, or when stuck in gridlock, the real work of awakening can begin. Although the Alzheimer's patient and the DP are the perfect embodiment—examples that are well-known and easily recognized—any moderately difficult person will readily demonstrate a chronic resistance pattern and can act as your perfect mental mirror.

When we are able to observe another's noisy mind, we can train ourselves to notice the same in ourselves, even if it is to a lesser degree. Once the patterns of compulsive, dysfunctional minds are seen for what they are—a negative feeding frenzy of unconscious objection to one thing after another—it's hard to return to ignorance. Finally, spiritual growth becomes possible because the cloak of denial has been lifted.

Everyone can improve. Very few dare to fine-tune themselves to a degree that they cause no further emotional harm to themselves or others. This level of mastery is of an entirely different order than simply mollifying the ego through self-improvement techniques or therapies. Spiritual mastery, by being present in the moment, when chronic emotional reactivity has ceased, is not only a blessed gift to self and others, but it is exactly what is needed when the whole world is crying for peace. Only a person with a quiet mind is able to contribute to community or planetary peace on any lasting scale, because it is the noisy mind that ensures that world suffering remains so pervasive. The global initiative of peace must begin individually "in this moment."

In the same way that a wilderness mountaineering guide would instruct his group to "leave no trace," the ultimate gift to those around us—the highest expression of love—is to do the same with our noisy and compulsive mind. Lack of mental noise is enlightenment. This new level of mastery is possible for everyone and is no longer reserved for a monastic few. Those free of chronic negative thought must become the normal state of being for the majority in order for the planet to survive. At the very least, it's the only assurance of lasting peace within interpersonal relationships. It is only within an environment of peace, whether at home, the workplace, or within a community, that each person's full and true purpose can be activated and realized. Despite a common misunderstanding, the noisy, compulsive mind contributes little to any dynamic or enterprise that has any real lasting value.

One of the most prevalent characteristics of a noisy mind is the way that it compulsively weighs in on the circumstances that arise in the present moment and chronically objects to it, no matter what that is. Once, while stopped at a stoplight, Jeannette demanded that I drive through the intersection. "The light is red," I calmly responded. Jeannette didn't understand and repeated her command, this time with more force and anger. Her hands waved angrily in front of her, motioning for me to get the car going. "The traffic light is still red. I'm waiting for it to turn green." Still not understanding, Jeannette reached out to honk the horn so that the car in front of us would move out of our way. Without admonishment, I raised my arm to gently block her, and she was stunned into silence by the lack of any emotion in my response. This inner "presence" she could feel. It has a way of stopping the noisy mind in its tracks. By the time the light had turned green, her discontent arose again, and I could observe the mechanics of her mind as it unconsciously sought a way to seduce a negative reaction in me. This interplay of negative reaction between people is what the DP most effectively invokes and is why such havoc is created in their immediate environment. The DP actually needs to complain and suffer, the reason for which is explained in detail in the next few chapters.

After traveling about a mile or two down Pacific Coast Highway, Jeannette opened the window of the car and threw out a handful of trash, knowing for certain (although on an unconscious level) that this would get a reaction. After pulling over to the side of the road, I gathered the trash and tossed it back into the car, with a firm yet calm command that littering would not be tolerated. As we continued on our way, Jeannette unbuckled her seat belt, which prompted me to advise her to rebuckle it. She ignored me.

As a result, I pulled over once again to the side of the road and parked, turning off the engine. "We're not driving until you fasten your seatbelt." She clenched her fists at me, threatening to strike. She yelled that this was her car and that I had no right to order her around in her own car. With my spiritual practice firmly in place, my serenity was secure, and I was unmoved by her tantrum. Calmly observing the beauty of the wind in the trees and even commenting to her about it while she raged, I felt the deepest gratitude to have been released from the chronic mental suffering that had so thoroughly taken over Jeannette. Eventually, she fastened her seatbelt and we continued on our journey.

The analytical mind is completely unaware of the perfection of universal intelligence, that awesome force that conspires in the convergence of happenings, circumstances, events, and occurrences arising seemingly out of nowhere to reveal life's innate harmony. Although the analytical mind has served some purpose in moving the human species forward in its evolution, its use has surpassed its original function and is now moving the species in the reverse direction, toward its own extinction. It is the analytical mind that is behind chronic faultfinding and its insistent objections, which, when taken to a global scale, explains war and genocide.

There is indeed a perfection to universal intelligence. But because the mind senses that this "web of coincidence" is beyond anyone's ability to control or manipulate it, the mind responds with an attempt to reinstate a counterfeit superiority. It does so simply through its loud, obnoxious, and chronic objection to what *is*. And this defiance of the present moment is considered by most people to be a normal way of reacting to life's flow.

This is also the near-chronic state of mind demonstrated by those with Alzheimer's or dementia or by any DP. That is why it is so helpful to be in their close proximity. If you want to see how you operate, just observe the DP's mind. The functioning of your own mind will hardly be any quieter. The only difference is one of degree. Whereas the unafflicted person may still be able to surrender to the pressure of maintaining social norms to some degree, they may not do so in the privacy of their own home, which is why bitter negativity often occurs behind closed doors.

Micromanaging one's surroundings and other people and circumstances are the classic symptoms of an extremely noisy and compulsive mind. This person is often referred to as being a "perfectionist." In actual fact, there is no perfection ever found in or created by a compulsive mind which is habitually focused on minutia. Indeed, the perfectionist hasn't yet matured spiritually enough to recognize that the only action which creates a sense of perfect completeness is an inner movement of allowance. A perfectionist's outer attempts at correcting their environment are a chronic need to remain compulsively identified with so-called problems. It is minutia-focus at its most extreme.

A noisy mind cannot accept the ebb and flow of life. It cannot surrender to the instability of all forms. It admonishes any change out of hand. Without a spiritual context, the mind is allowed to run rampant, chronically complaining and correcting minutia. The mind cannot tolerate the recognition that life has its own natural flow. The noisy mind is in abject denial of the true present moment.

The present moment is right now. It is not to be confused with the *circumstances* that arise in the moment. It is this slice of right now that is the perfectly simple peaceful life *underneath* the content. It's the stillness in the background of a well-furnished house being decorated for a party. The present moment is not the furniture or the people or the birthday celebration inside that house. Instead, it is the beauty and perfection of the lovely quiet that exists despite the noisy party chatter. The present moment is the animating life that makes the house and the party possible.

Imagine a powerful river winding through hundreds, or even thousands of miles of countryside. It crosses varying terrains of forest, desert, and prairie, until reaching the sea. At its source, perhaps at the mighty rainforests of the Amazon, several small twigs drop from a branch, floating to the middle of the river. The twigs, although embraced by the mighty foaming water, become part of the river, as they are carried along.

One of the twigs becomes washed ashore along the bank of the forest. A second twig settles in the mud as the river branches at the desert. Yet another of the twigs continues for many thousands of miles. It has no idea where it will be delivered, or upon which bank it will settle. The wise twig appreciates the changing seasons, and changing terrain, as it's carried along, knowing that ultimately the timing of its destination is beyond its control. The wise twig knows that the river of life, although mysterious in its way and manner, can be trusted to support the twig toward its ultimate destination. The ebb and flow of the river, the entire zigzag of the twig's journey, are recognized as a force of nature beyond its ken.

Imagine how absurd it would be if one of the twigs struggled to get out of the water and decided that it wanted to change the course of the river. So, instead of floating downstream from the forest to the desert, it wanted the river's course to flow back to the rainforest. If the twig were to fly into a furious fit and yell at the river for its indifference, it would be demonstrating normal human behavior when responding to the present moment. In its anger and resistance, it pushes at the river's bank in a futile attempt to change its meandering course.

*It is insanity of the highest order to become angry or resistant to something that already is.*

When a person has a negative emotional reaction to an event or circumstance *that has* already *happened*, he can be said to be "pushing the river."

Of course, change can still be initiated and improvements implemented, but they are done calmly and peacefully without negative emotional reactions and in harmony with the greater whole. Reacting angrily to something that already *is,* is the normal mental pattern of just about everyone. The only exception is the person who is awakening spiritually and becomes conscious of their own mental patterns.

Discharging wanton negative reactions practically personifies the essence of the emotional state of the Alzheimer's or dementia patient or DP. They become fully lost in their reactions and resistance to just about everything. When a DP discharges anger aimed at others, although they are simultaneously expressing that they are suffering, they actually experience enormous deep pleasure. Once this unconscious yearning for drama is recognized in others, it is more easily recognized in oneself. Even when a DP in your environment is not interested or unable to make any conscious changes toward improvement, your own growth in this area is all that is needed as you tend to your own garden first. Once planted, what blossoms and how those blossoms affect your environment will astound you.

DPs do not need drama, however, when their noisy mind is in the active stage of augmenting itself through accumulation or material gain, or an increase in status or recognition. Since the noisy mind is inherently dissatisfied, it is in a constant state of searching out strategies for self-enhancement. The reason is that it is the ego aspect of the person that is in need of gaining something—the division of the psyche that concerns itself with conceit, self-esteem, and self-respect. In contrast, your inner essence or being needs nothing outside itself to feel deeply peaceful and satisfied.

To the contrary, the ego, or egoic mind, is habitually insecure and lives in fear of the past and of the future. That's all it knows. That's why it can never, ever tolerate the present moment, because its survival is in question. In the case of the person who is awakening spiritually, this is an initial challenge until enough momentum is created, and why the mind shuns quiet and seeks habitual minutia of existence on which to focus. The mind adopts all manner of predictable strategies to get "you" to focus on what "it" says is important: the past or the future, problems or problematic people, or absent these, a compulsive focus on meaningless minutia.

It is no accident that almost anyone in the presence of an Alzheimer's patient or DP immediately begins to flatter them, in whatever form that takes. This is because most people instinctively recognize that these people have lost their depth of perception and exist in the shallow surface of existence in which the ego rules. And yet, most of us are unaware that we, too, flounder in this shallow pool of perception, allowing our noisy minds to chase compliments and to habitually identify weaknesses in others.

The egoic mind, with its meaningless pursuits, seeks evidence of its superiority, and if it can't find any, simply objects to what *is*. This objection serves to create a sense of moral superiority. The goal has been achieved. The ego is boosted and is set to defend itself.

The Alzheimer's patient and DP are often characterized by uncontrolled outbursts of rage. Yet when we look more closely at ourselves, we can see this pattern alive in us too. We will notice our own compulsive objections to the present moment, and our own demand that something that *is,* should not be. We will see our need to gain others' approval and acceptance—the reasons why our ego's sense of dignity is so easily shaken. And when challenged, the noisy mind, by definition, is quick to anger.

If you want to see this pattern alive in yourself, you can see it clearly by observing how angry outbursts in another—whether an Alzheimer's or dementia patient, the DP, or in someone unafflicted—become temporarily lessened when the ego is flattered. However seemingly effective this technique is in softening their rage, flattery does not reduce the egoic discharge when used as an attempt to control mood. The reason is that the noisy mind has become *identified* with possessions, bodies, attributes, or roles; and as such, these identifications—the root cause of their suffering—become strengthened, rather than softened, by the flattery.

True healing begins to emerge when a caregiver or family member, instead of coaxing an angry person out of a mood through flattery, instead adopts a still alert state of awareness and simply "holds" that quiet awareness while the other's noisy mind acts out. This is called aligning with presence. Once in my third year, when Jeannette was very angry with me for some minor reason, she approached me with a fist as if she was going to strike me. By this time, I was deeply grounded in presence, and as she came right up to my face, I looked deeply into her eyes without any mental commentary of my own. Feeling at complete serenity, I stood there facing her for a minute or two, until she seemed to simply decide to turn away.

When you meet a DP while grounded in your own presence, your peace often dissolves their anger and does not add further escalation to the negative energy of the cycle. Sometimes, however, the DP, momentarily thwarted, will return again later with a new stronger tactic to draw you in; but even then, if met with your own stillness once more, the cycle is on its way to permanent dissolution. Any commentary should help the DP recognize that there is an abiding peace alive within them, too, if they simply place their attention there. If your DP is in a tirade over some triviality, you can calmly refute their upset—that in and of itself the thing actually holds no power to disrupt or to cause suffering. You simply don't agree with its inherent ability to cause suffering. Do you recognize this distinction?

In other words, when Jeannette wails in protest during a tubal feeding, it may seem that it's important to "acknowledge her pain." In some psychological therapies, this is taught as a useful tool in dealing with someone who is upset. However, in so doing, you are unwittingly agreeing that the nightmare is true; when in actual fact, it is only by waking up from its hypnotic spell that the DP can recognize that the cause of the upset cannot in actual fact create suffering. Only the resistance to something can create suffering. This is the way you can truly help someone to dis-identify with whatever is being defended, whether it is the other's possessions, body, attributes, or roles, and not unwittingly contribute to their further alignment with it. Of course, words of compassion or compliments can still be generously given, but not as a means to manipulate or lessen mean or angry moods by acknowledging their upset or anger.

The way in which you can assist another in dis-identifying with their roles, attributes, or forms is to speak to the inner being underneath the noisy mind. You address the changeless essence or being of the person, not the impermanent trivialities so honored by the "diseased" mind. For example, instead of supporting a chronic focus on fashionable clothes or outer appearances, you instead bring attention to that state of peace and well-being that is already there under the mental objections without any need for adding things of form. Sometimes while with family, Jeannette will suddenly react with angry force to some benign event or comment, and her family members naturally look for ways to respond that will calm her down. This is when flattery for the sake of mitigating her tirade actually strengthens her habit rather than to slowly dissolve it.

A better and more lasting response is to calmly bring awareness to the perfection or natural beauty of peace and stillness that is already present in the room or the environment in order to help the DP to associate with it, rather than the nightmare that they have created in their own mind. While there is immense power that animates the life force, it nonetheless is still and quiet. It seems counterintuitive to bring attention to something that is still, quiet, and peaceful in the midst of a cyclone of madness; however, try it and you will see how effective it is. Simply place your own attention, and then bring in your DP's, on the perfection of a daisy growing in the garden or the loveliness of the wind blowing in the trees or the lovely quiet of the moment. The idea here is to focus their attention on the pervasive perfection of peace and stillness and replace the chronic need to pick apart and identify seeming imperfections. Simultaneously, while you are grounded in an everlasting peace, you can with authority remind others that what seems to be causing so much upset really doesn't matter that much and in fact is, more often than not, minutia focus, plain and simple. However, it is important for you to be authentically present, abiding and firmly grounded in your own peace. It is one's presence that animates the spoken words, not the actual words themselves, and thus it is the true source of the rippling effect of peace.

When we tell a terminally ill patient that she is okay with the right intent, it may seem that this is dishonest; however, we are not speaking to the mind's idea of what being "okay" means. We are addressing the inner being underneath the mind's shallow definition of its clinging safety net, which never guaranteed it anyway. When you are grounded in your own peaceful serenity, your encouraging words are absolutely true because you yourself have aligned with the peace that underlies and animates all form, a peace that is the other's natural state, too. Safety is inherently present because each being is more than a body, and as such, is forever part of the river of life. We may not understand it or agree with it, but we nonetheless have no ultimate power over it.

So when we respond to a person who is out of control emotionally, we can come to a state of presence and speak to the inner being, calmly but assuredly, reminding them that whatever the source of their upset, it has no importance. But when we respond this way, we do not simultaneously "acknowledge their pain." For example, if Jeannette begins to moan loudly and strike the dashboard because we are stuck in traffic, I respond calmly and assuredly that we are just fine, that the heavy traffic cannot hurt or harm us in any way, and that there is nowhere else we need to be. If necessary, this can be repeated two dozen times, slowly and calmly, in response to her renewed complaining. I do not simultaneously "acknowledge" that, yes, I know you don't like to sit in gridlock, but it will be over soon. This has the effect of telling the noisy mind that yes of course, any person can relate to this type of problem. Instead, no matter what, we do not agree that trivia has any power to disrupt or harm. Some of the most dramatic examples of Jeannette's busy mind literally stopping in its tracks and reaching stillness is when, responding to her tirade of impatience, I ask her, "Where are we rushing to?"

Strangely enough, when responding to a DP's tirade in this way, it has been my experience that others actually think of it as an "insensitive" response. We are so brainwashed by the culture's service to the noisy complaining mind, that to operate differently and refute a need to complain, seems unkind. When we deny or refuse to align with misery, we invite the highest possible recognition. Extremely disabled children, who grow to be highly functional as adults despite their physical limitations, often credit their parents who never capitulated to the mind's need for pity. During bouts of fury, we can gently assure others instead that they are safe and will be okay. If this needs to be repeated a dozen times while the angry person pursues a tirade, then so be it. You remain unmoved by temper tantrums and address the peace that "passeth all understanding." Bring attention to the peace that is already there underneath their foul temper and so-called problems.

For example, during tubal feedings, Jeannette would get a glimpse of the syringes and fly into a fit because she didn't want to be fed that way. Sometimes she could be distracted by some triviality, but not always. At those times, others would attempt to distract her by flattering her, trying to appease her rage; however, Jeannette's underlying resistance would seem to redouble the next day. Although it appeared that flattery seduced her anger into momentary silence, it did not provide an effective handling over the long term, in the same way that giving crack to an addict may seem to work for the moment. In the long run, a saner and effective solution was needed in order to prevent the patient's (or any DP's) dysfunctional mind patterns from holding the entire household hostage.

When Jeannette would try to scratch me or would attempt to throw something, a calm but firm response like quickly holding her wrist and telling her "No!" usually persuaded her that she wasn't getting her way; however, without a strong abiding alignment with the peace inherent in the true present, any words uttered are void of healing power. It is the stillness underneath the chaotic exterior that sources any miracle of healing, even when that healing is as simple as the slow but steady dissolution of your DP's tendency to rage. With Jeannette, once my own stillness is accessed, then I can confidently insert the syringe into the feeding tube, even when her defiant physical reaction is possible. This sets up a more appropriate context so that the DP recognizes that their anger cannot seduce your reaction.

It was a constant source of insight to observe the way Jeannette's mind so fervently rebuked attempts to feed her via the tube. Because of her strong identification with her former beauty and physical athleticism, the mere sight of me approaching her with syringes of Ensure would often initiate intense fury and loathsomeness. There were times when she would grab my finger and bend it backward, as though she were trying to break it. And yet, where was the problem? The tubal feedings caused no pain or discomfort. She was warm, clothed, beautifully housed, surrounded by caring loved ones, with no financial concerns whatsoever. This is not in any way meant to mitigate her intense emotional suffering which brought out the compassion of those close to her. It was, however, her intense reaction to what *is* that provided an example of where we all go awry. It's simply a noisy mind making up the rules as it goes, as to what's acceptable and what's not.

Of course, you might say to yourself, "Yes, but I have financial concerns," or, "*I* have real pain and discomfort." But in the thin slice of now, in just this present moment, is there any problem? There can *be* no problem in the present moment. There may be things to handle, decisions to be made, pain to be surrendered to, or challenges to overcome. But in this moment of now, all is okay. The stillness and perfection of what *is*, when finally observed through a quiet mind, is all that ultimately matters and the balm that cures all.

An often-frequent response to the idea of accepting the present moment as it *is*, is to misunderstand how it actually works in real life. It does not mean that you must do what others want you to do, or to accept the unacceptable. Instead, you behold what *is*. In the event you are with a DP, observe the temper tantrum calmly and accept that it is indeed here in the moment of now. *Then,* respond calmly and effectively.

Part of that response may involve commanding a high quality "No!" which may occur quite often. But that "No" is not imbued with anger, resistance, hurt feelings, or upset. Magically, a high quality "No!" brings more authority with it, although it may be delivered much quieter. It emerges from a deepening motivation for peace, rather than an unconscious movement for control. This quality, although seemingly indistinguishable from its opposite, is actually quite palpable as being associated with trust on a deep, invisible level. Although most people would not be able to identify why, at the deepest level, they can sense when an individual truly has no underlying motivation to gain an advantage.

This is not to suggest that Jeannette always approved of me. This was hardly the case. What it means is that, despite her ups and downs between fond trust and resentment of me, my role as caregiver is anchored to the present moment. This anchoring allows me to stay clear and unmoved during her frequent displays of mistrust and opposition. My own ability to remain anchored to peace allowed Jeannette to uncover her own inner self, which offset her ego's response by slowly dissolving it. This is an ideal way of being in the world, as we all encounter others' ever-changing opinions of us.

Because each of us is suffering from the nightmare of believing that mostly outward things and circumstances can help or heal us, in order to really help someone, we must bring their attention to their true essence. When we practice aligning with presence ourselves, we most help the DP to connect to the eternal part of them that *is* never changing: their true essence, the inner essence that brings the body to life. It is the same essence that is in the warm winds of summer and the dolphins that breach at sunset. And which emanates from a person or caregiver aligning with presence.

Even when a person who is awakened spiritually is in fast motion, such as when rushing here and there within the house tending to the terminally ill patient's urgent bodily needs, the presence that empowers that particular expression of life is completely and utterly *still*. If ever there is a myth that can be joyously abandoned, it is the idea that in order to feel deep peace, one's body must be quiet, alone, and meditating. To the contrary, the student of spirituality who actually puts their practice into effect can have a very busy body, attending to multiple responsibilities and urgent demands, but can do so in the context of absolute inner serenity. You can still race to the other side of the room to urgently administer the Heimlich maneuver to the choking victim, but your fast action is animated by perfect quiet and stillness at its core. A quiet mind leads the way and sets the tone of the body despite its busyness. In this way, a still mind aligns perfectly with the true present moment, because they are virtually indistinguishable. Even the noisy mind is only able to exist by what sources it: the still, quiet life force from within.

*This life force is also the same "thing" as the present moment.*

This concept is so difficult for most people to understand that it will be addressed again later. In the meantime, consider that the deepest, truest statement that can be made about the nature of a person is that at their essence, they *are* the present moment. Of course, neither the life force nor the present moment is a "thing." In fact, they are quite the opposite, which is a "no thing" or space. Space is stillness. This is why aligning with it is so healing and so potentially powerful. Observe any peaceful being, whether an animal, quiet-minded person, or a wildflower. Notice how fully it exists in the now. You too, share this alignment with the present moment, although when obscured by noisy thought, you don't have an awareness of it. This is another way that, by observing another being, although a quiet-minded one, you can see the same lovely essence in yourself.

Once, many years ago, when I was a young mother deeply upset and in the throes of a divorce, a mystical vision appeared in the middle of the night in which a spiritual master stood at the foot of my bed. Hardly able to contain my awe and surprise, I sensed a palpable peaceful essence that emanated from him and inspired me to achieve a similar state over the next twenty years. Although he said nothing, it was his lovely stillness, yet so powerful in its creative force, that spoke the loudest. In that moment, I became aware of what was possible, for he embodied humanity's potential: to exist in an unshakeable peace that became for me the only truly meaningful goal in life. This chronic state of well-being became my most fervent desire and fueled the events and decisions that have shaped my life since that moment.

The present moment is this slice of now. It is the still, nothingness out of which circumstances arise, but it is of itself, always still and peaceful. Some people may better relate to the idea of the present moment as the soul or spirit of a person. Indeed, the invisible essence that underlies and animates life is the same as the soul. It is the precise essence that comprises the deepest part of any living being. Hence, the still, present moment is the same thing as the deepest essence of *you*. That is why when you are able to rest peacefully without resistance despite the circumstances of the present moment, you are healed. That is why the noisy egoic mind will never get you to peace because *its* nature is loud and obnoxious.

When we recognize that resistance to the present moment can be the only real problem, suddenly, all so-called problems can be reduced by simply being mentally still. Suddenly, there are no problems. There are only challenges that can be addressed in the present moment. This distinction changes everything.

If there are really no real problems at all, then why does a noisy mind obliterate the perfection of a quiet peace? The answer is, it doesn't. It only obscures it until your inner essence becomes aware of the stillness underneath the chronic noisiness, and "brings it back" through your awareness of it. This is yet another apparent dichotomy at work: you can be in a noisy crowded room and still align perfectly with the quiet moment of now that resides underneath the chaos. That stillness underneath all the material objects is the ever-present perfection of peace. This is life itself.

The most effective antidote to an angry or mean-spirited outburst by another is meeting the person imbued in this still, loving life force. It creates a force field of sorts that affects everything around it. This assists the person in dis-identifying with their behavior. In essence, you would present peace as an offering to them by your own example as this peace flows into the other. In speaking to Jeannette, my nonresistance to her rage diminishes the ego in her and helps her to become aware of the still presence within herself. Any stride she may make in this area mitigates her suffering. Any words that are spoken to a DP from the state of quiet stillness, by their very nature, are imbued with the same essence and are healing, not manipulative. Exactly how it is possible to quiet the mind is described later.

It sounds so simple, this idea of consciously aligning with the present moment, by refraining from commenting on or rejecting the "badness" of what shows up. We can all recognize these patterns when they arise in the Alzheimer's or dementia patient or the DP. But can we recognize them in ourselves? If you look deeply, you will notice characteristics of chronic objection demonstrated in you and everybody else. This is considered a normal way of reacting to life's ups and downs. It seems that only the mentally afflicted have crossed over into an exaggerated demonstration of this pathology. But from a spiritual perspective, a distinction between the behavior of an Alzheimer's mind, a DP, a squealing three year old, and a "normal" mind is practically nonexistent.

The Alzheimer's patient and DP can be observed to react angrily or in disgust at the slightest provocation. Perhaps it's raining. Perhaps it's too sunny. Maybe the patient is in a waiting room of a doctor's office and the doctor is running late, and they are angry, unable to tolerate anything that interferes with previously made plans or schedules. We all demonstrate an inability to be at peace with the true present moment when we search for a way to keep our mind busy. Maybe we get on the phone in order to distract ourselves, all in an effort to avoid what *is*. Clever means of avoidance of the now, or multitasking, are still an inability to tolerate what *is*. And remember, when you are intolerant of what shows up, you are shouting "No!" to the river of life. You are pushing the river upstream and have lost equanimity. In its place, negative mental noise takes residence and suffering is guaranteed.

The reason this habit of reactivity is so useless is that negative reactions themselves do not change what *is*. The "is-ness" is before you. The river of life has taken a twisting turn at the prairie. Yet in our culture, most people are out on the riverbank pushing the river in defiance. This is the time to behold what *is*, and accept it. Then, once accepted, you can make other arrangements or change your plans, but *after* you settle into a peaceful allowing of this interruption. This is the way that the mature student of spirituality allows the circumstances of life to be their sacred spiritual practice, rather than limiting a time of "sacred worship" to when you are in church, synagogue, yoga class, etc.

The reason why we have all become so habituated into reacting, condemning, criticizing, and complaining has to do with the cancerous-like growth of the egoic mind, which makes it appear as if every single person on Earth has full-blown dementia. This is because most mental characteristics are shared by everyone and most can't see beyond that.

The good news is that there is a simple and effective practice that can assist the Alzheimer's patient, the DP, upset children, and the student of spirituality who are trapped in their mental environment. When adopted, an amazing, transformative essence of life emerges from their pathological state of mind. Suddenly, there is peace. Out of this peace, changes can be initiated, and now Heaven on Earth can be realized.

But before you can muster the discipline or interest in applying the antidote, it helps to first understand the mechanics of the monster we need to tame and what its own purpose is.

3

---

# The Nature of the Beast

THE MIND WANTS YOU DEAD.

This statement may come as a surprise since you may have assumed that you are your mind. Instead, you are an immortal being who has a mind that can be used for practical purposes and then put away until it's needed again; however, the role of the mind has grown out of control and has actually taken over the host, or you. In the same way that a cunning and manipulative servant can overrun the master of the house, the mind now pretends to be you, and has you subservient to it.

To imply that some "part" of you wants you dead may sound extreme. And yet, uncovering the actual dynamic of what is in fact taking place is the beginning of your ability to unravel its hold on you. If this idea sounds preposterous, than you have missed the essence of the actual depth and degree of the way and manner that the analytical mind has taken over you. If you look and listen deeply to the teachings of any awakened spiritual teacher, including Eckhart Tolle, you will encounter this precise message, although perhaps softened a bit so as not to offend;

however, should you go more deeply into their teachings, you will no doubt find clues as to the true breadth of disruption leveled by the analytical mind on its host. Because you desire to awaken consciously—rather than as a result of near suicide and intense mental suffering as was the case with Eckhart Tolle or Byron Katie—then it is extraordinarily helpful to begin to recognize the exact cunning and disruptive nature of your own mind.

The conscious process to self-realization is a virtually brand new development in human evolution. It therefore requires a new recognition, namely, that the "voice" of this most devious and destructive analytical mind cannot be trusted nor relied upon. Indeed, this book endeavors to bring to your awareness actual clues as to precisely how and when your mind's voice is pretending to be you. The egoic thought structure, as it now exists through eons of evolution, has far outlived its initial purpose, and in fact is on a reverse vector to ensure chaos and demise. This cannot be sugarcoated or stated softly. Even though it means the eventual demise of itself, the analytical mind exists to disrupt, tear apart, and eventually destroy your essence. Of course, ultimately this is not possible, because one's true essence is synonymous with the source of life; in fact, you are life. This is the essence of you, not your mind.

The mind is a tool that is animated and made possible by you, or your soul essence. But when the mind grows in such importance that it starts to pretend to be you, your essence becomes obscured, and in its place this near-demon wreaks havoc because it does not have sufficient character or spiritual maturity to be more than a servant. With its usurped power, it's literally a monster run amok.

Of course, this sounds outrageous, but almost no one questions the way and manner that this servant has entirely taken over every aspect of the household because it's so normal. When a person can be observed to quickly switch from gentle to mean-spirited, it can be said that the mind has usurped "you" and if unchecked will establish itself as in charge. You often hear parents say, "You were so sweet as a child," or before the mind took over in adolescence and the child became a teenage terror.

Because it is so rare to observe the way and manner that the mind has obscured your inner essence, when you do finally take notice, the mind senses an attack and wants you out of the way; or, if you can tolerate knowing the actual way of it, it wants you dead.

When this situation is recognized, a direct path to peace becomes possible because finally, the master of the house realizes how the servant has been allowed to dominate and create dysfunction. With this recognition, steps can be taken, described in the following chapters, that return the mind to its proper role as a tool, rather than a tyrant.

If the mind is not the same as your true essence, it would seem then that you have been split in two. What has really occurred is that the still, quiet, powerful true essence of you has been covered up. The degree to which your essence is obscured equals the degree of difficulty in living or being around you. If your essence is almost entirely obscured, then the people around you suffer in the extreme because the mind has no natural ability in dealing with the circumstances that arise in the present moment. This is why the mind, when it's chronically noisy, insists upon focusing on the past or the future, or on meaningless minutia.

When given any status other than that of a tool (its most benign state), the mind acts as though a person has turned over the reins of ruling a country to a self-centered and ignorant teenager. Naturally, chaos will become the norm. In its most disruptive state, the mind is nasty, aggressive, and mean spirited—a true demon. This whole idea may seem strange, especially when the mind conducting the tyranny is very intelligent; however, we're not bestowing special status on a brilliant mind with particular ability to solve puzzles and orchestrate thoughts to solve problems. Our discussion involves the usurping of the essence of a being by a tyrannical mind, whether or not the mind is smart or of average intelligence. In fact, often, the smarter the mind, the more havoc it wreaks—professionally, interpersonally, and spiritually.

The essence of *you* and your mind have two vastly different goals. The mind exists to prove that problems abound and to get *you* to stay focused on *them*. If there aren't any problems on which to focus, the mind will create some. *You*—the essence of you— needs nothing to feel complete since you are already deeply satisfied as the creative life force that animates everything. In fact, you and life are synonymous. Imagine asking a cloud what it needs to feel better. There's nothing that can be added by any kind of solid matter or form that would improve upon its beingness as a cloud. The same is true for you. Despite cultural conditioning to the contrary, you are complete as you are. Once self-realization occurs by dissolving all that obstructs right perception, you will know this to be true.

As soon as your inner essence—or as Eckhart Tolle has coined the term, *"presence"*—begins to take note of the dysfunctional patterns at work, the mind easily recognizes that its days may be numbered. Because it is narcissistic in the extreme, it doesn't want to be demoted to the role of a tool; it adores the power of tyranny. This is when it attempts to reinstate its dominance by refuting that effective spiritual practice actually has any merit. And then, because you're habituated into believing everything the mind thinks, you believe that it's gospel. This point will be discussed again and again because it is not easy to awaken from your hypnotic state when the hypnotist prefers that you slumber.

Putting into place simple but effective spiritual practice enables this presence to be reclaimed fully, which guarantees an immediate flourishing on all fronts. It's as if all your telephone lines to life have been blocked and suddenly are opened, and everybody and everything are talking to you again; however, this communication is imbued with stillness not noisiness as you shift your awareness from a focus on chaos, to a focus on the quiet that underlies all of life. Ironically, you begin to recognize that the stillness holds all solutions.

As you awaken from this hypnotic slumber, your inherently powerful and creative presence is targeted for deactivation by the mind. Since the inner essence of you is complete in and of itself, needing nothing outside itself for a sense of completion, anything added is by the part of the mind that is in a chronic state of needing and wanting: the ego. As was discussed previously, the ego is concerned with self-seeking and upholding its identity. As normal as this may seem in our culture, an enlightened being does not concern himself with his reputation and other people's opinions (opinions that arise from *their* egoic minds).

By its very nature, the egoic mind structure can never, ever be satisfied for any length of time because it is comprised of a false identity without any foundation. It virtually exists to find myriad ways to enhance itself and to use egoic reflection via others' compliments and by trying to stand out and become special in order to sustain itself.

To clarify, there is nothing wrong with having material possessions, to strive for goals and to accomplish projects, and to become educated. The distinguishing factor here is whether or not you become *lost* in it. For example, should you lose things due to stock market declines, bank failures, divorce, etc., or lose status or physical agility due to age or failing health, only the person who has *not* become identified with such will not crash emotionally. It is this identification with something owned, earned, or fostered that creates suffering when lost.

During the early stages of Jeannette's Alzheimer's, although her cognition was still quite intact, it was not safe for her to operate a car. Once she had backed into a pole and another time she had phoned home saying that she was lost. Of course, she objected vehemently to any suggestion that she should relinquish her driver's license, insisting that anyone could have made such mistakes. Despite her diagnosis, she demanded that empirical evidence be presented before she would agree to stop driving her beloved new convertible.

At her husband's request, and after making a few calls, I discovered a local hospital that conducts just such a driving test that is geared for dementia patients in order to privately assess their driving ability. The driving part of the test is done virtually. This provides a way to assess driving ability without turning dementia patients loose on the streets of Los Angeles with an unsuspecting test proctor from the Department of Motor Vehicles. For several weeks prior to the test, Jeannette studied her booklet, nervous but determined that she would pass.

She didn't. Her impaired mind could not quickly process all the decisions needed when a driver approaches a busy intersection, maneuvers freeway acceleration lanes, or beholds children or animals on the road. To say that she was emotionally devastated hardly describes her mood for the next year. She was inconsolably angry and tearful, and it became an ongoing cat and mouse game as she would try to find or grab the keys to her car. Her family felt that it would be less devastating to temporarily refrain from selling it altogether, but when an outing was required to the doctor or grocery store, I chauffeured her in her car. She would not agree to be a passenger in mine.

One day she found her keys. Speeding out of the driveway like a NASCAR driver late for a race, she left me in the dust before I could stop her. She proceeded to drive down to the local shopping center while I remained at home and tracked her whereabouts on the computer via satellite tracking. Concerned that one day she just might find the keys, we had previously installed a tracking device in the car for just this reason.

On her way down the street, several neighbors spotted her and phoned, wondering if I was asleep on the job. Many neighbors were friends of the family, and they knew that Jeannette was not supposed to be driving. After explaining that she had found the keys in their hiding place, we all formed a plan to "capture" our errant runaway before she caused a multicar pileup.

We successfully returned her home but not without high drama. She continually shouted and pointed at the shiny Mercedes yelling that it belonged to *her*. So much of her identity was caught up in owning and driving it. Despite assurances that she would be driven anywhere she wanted to go, at any time, day or night, she was unmoved by this accommodation. It was her car, she repeated vehemently, and if she couldn't drive it, she wanted to kill herself.

Most of us can relate, at least to some degree, to how upsetting this must be for dementia patients, or even for the handicapped. The loss of a driver's license is often equated with loss of freedom. But is this really what freedom *is?* As I observed her ongoing tirades about this for over a year, drawing in her family and friends' sympathetic reactions, Jeannette's emotional dilemma provoked in me further deep inner searching. Was this what life was about: driving cars to shopping malls; driving cars to jobs; driving cars to see more cars? While I had grown up in L.A.'s mobile culture with the slogan, "You're only as good as your car," I could now see the insanity of it: this idea that a lump of metal and glass had anything to do with our state of being. "We are all seriously deranged," I concluded, recognizing how I, too, have been all too attached to objects and stuff.

As was mentioned previously, it is just this type of identification with something owned, earned, or fostered that creates suffering when lost. This example of Jeannette's car and driver's license is exactly what it means to thoroughly *identify* with something. If any such a "thing" is conceived to be *part* of you, of course suffering occurs when it's lost. This recognition helped me to develop and implement a successful spiritual practice to handle this type of identification with roles, forms, and attributes. It is described later in chapter 7.

When self-realization occurs, this normal way of relating to shiny junk is recognized as folly. It may be hard to believe right now, but it is possible to enjoy the fruits of a material world, and yet be absolutely unmoved at the reality of relinquishing all of those fruits as a result of any kind of loss.

*Nonidentification with form and alignment with presence is the only healthy way to conceive of ownership while living in a material world in which things don't last very long.*

When you are fully aligned with your inner source, you can be said to be self-realized. The self-realized person is fully conscious of their true nature as an immortal being and thus cannot get lost in the dream that any kind of form is supposed to be permanent. (This also applies to so-called "immortalists" who want to remain in the same body forever.) The self-realized person has identified with presence, rather than form, and so seeks more of it—stillness and quiet—in order to recharge themselves, rather than running to piles of metal and glass (sports cars) or other material objects.

The seeker, on the way to self-realization, recognizes the nature of the beast, but dares to consciously align and identify with its opposite. Stillness and the present moment and *you* are all the same "thing." In order to know *you* more fully, allow its opposite to drop away: all the noisy mind's objections to effective spiritual practice that ensures your peace. This is the nature of the beast: the mind that objects to the source of its undoing. Since the mind loathes the simplicity of now, and tries to make trouble by convincing you that there are instead many problems in the now, then the solution to putting the mind in its proper place as a tool is to align more fully with the present moment. When you do so, you are facing the beast, and dissolving it.

Since you cannot rely on things to give you happiness or long-term satisfaction, then the only appropriate attachment worth your reliance is the present moment. Only the present moment, the thin slice of now that underlies all circumstance and happenings, can be relied upon as a "safety mechanism" in which to know the truth of who you are. Ironically, only when aligning with the present moment can you know for certainty that no safety mechanism is needed. Again, the misconception of needing anything whatsoever for happiness or safety is what self-realization cures.

Jeannette, almost always leery of activity around her as a physical threat, reacted strongly to the sound of an ambulance, or even laughter, as evidence that she may be at risk in some way or evidence that she was excluded. As her cognition decreased, of course, to some degree she was excluded by virtue of her lack of understanding of conversations, etc.; however, even prior to her significant cognitive declines, already in place were her strong angry reactions of control wherein she demanded that others' actions and comments be approved by her. In the later stage, unless she was focused on some task, such as when she was coloring in her coloring book, she remained restless: searching in cupboards and drawers, looking for things hidden, repeatedly cleaning or straightening, listening in on telephone conversations, suspicious that she was unstable, unsafe, and on the outside looking in. In some ways, her early fears and subsequent attempts at chronic control of people and her environment were ironically made manifest through the onset of her late-stage condition.

Even if you were to agree that alignment with the present moment is potentially a more stable identification than to that of form, many people cannot readily comprehend what the present moment actually *is,* or at least how aligning with it can provide what is suggested. You may recognize the dysfunction of a noisy mind, and even notice its overbearing insistence on shunning simplicity and stillness; however, you may not be quite convinced that aligning fully with presence has any real practical application. So first, let's consider what the present moment is *not.*

Prior to my awakening, in celebration of Jeannette's forty-fifth wedding anniversary, Jeannette and her husband flew to Maui. They asked me to accompany them, because as Jeannette's full-time caregiver, not only did I manage the myriad tasks involved in administering her medications and dietary issues, but Jeannette was very comfortable with me by now. It was common for me to travel with them in order to help with her care and the management of the details of the trip.

One morning at the condo where we were staying, Jeannette's husband had to take a conference call on his cell phone in the adjoining room. Jeannette and I hung out in the kitchen and made breakfast. This was prior to the insertion of her feeding tube.

As was customary, suddenly, for no particular reason, Jeannette became irate and headed for the door. It is common for Alzheimer's patients to wander about as they suddenly get restless and simply leave the house, even if they don't know where they're going and are unfamiliar with their surroundings, due to their dementia. However, in this case, she had been to her condo in Maui many times, so she rushed out the door confidently. She beat me out the door and down the corridor to the elevators where she pushed the button. As her luck would have it, the doors opened immediately and then closed behind her, leaving me on the platform. I waited for a second elevator to arrive and on the ground floor immediately ran through the lobby looking for her. She was not in the lobby, or around the swimming pool. Other guests and hotel staff joined in the search. One person headed for the parking lot, another checked the beach where hundreds of people were playing in the surf or sunning themselves. Despite our best efforts, she had disappeared.

In this example, the present moment is *not* the missing person and *not* my beating heart as I run at top speed throughout the entire condo complex looking for her. The present moment is *not* the relief that I feel when I finally return to the condo twenty minutes later, and she is there. In this example, the present moment is the stillness underneath all that chaos, which included the stillness of essence inherent in the sun shining through the hallway window, the tranquil green plants in the lobby, and the sound of waves rolling onto the shore. It was the harmony of everybody just going about their business on another pleasant day in paradise. At any point in that drama, the peace and perfection of the present moment is accessible.

It appeared that she had gotten lost on one of the interim floors of the condo complex, then later had simply been able to find her way back to the correct floor, and ultimately to the right room.

Now back in the kitchen, we took up where we had left off with breakfast. Jeannette's French toast, now cooled, needed to be reheated, but she rebuffed my attempt to place it in the microwave. Instead, she took the paper plate and placed it on the stove's burner, then turned it on. Although I attempted to explain that the paper plate was catching on fire, she was determined to see this through to the end. When I took it off the stove, this pushed her into a rage. For no reason in particular, her response was to open the freezer and take out a bottle of frozen water; Jeannette wanted to pour the frozen water out, but of course, it didn't pour. When I attempted to intervene, it only further infuriated her; at which point, she grabbed a steak knife and began stabbing at the frozen bottle in order to free the frozen water. When I again attempted to intervene, she flew into a rage, dropped the knife, and headed out the door again. Suddenly, my nose started to bleed severely without warning, but there was no time to clean up.

This time, I made it into the elevator with her but she was inconsolably angry and poked every button on the panel. After several stops, eventually, the elevator made its way to the lobby, and she exited, irritated that I was accompanying her. Furiously waving me off, I nonetheless stayed with her, although a step or two behind, hoping that by giving her a little space, she would calm down.

Within an hour, her anger had dissipated, and we returned to the room. We were met by her husband, whose conference call had ended and who had wandered into the kitchen to look for us. Imagine his concern when he saw the steak knife, stabbed water bottle, and blood on the floor as he furiously dialed my cell phone to find out if we were okay.

In this example, the present moment is *not* any of the incidents in this story. The present moment cannot include any drama, because it is, by definition, very simple. It is the peaceful moment of "now" underneath the chaos.

*The present moment is not the story of you in the now. It is the now itself.*

If you become still and alert, you can hear it as the stillness underneath whatever is happening. As the old Simon and Garfunkel song goes, it's the "sound of silence." That is the present moment. There is nothing that's ever going wrong in the present moment because how can perfection be imperfect? If you disagree that the present moment is perfect, then you are not referring to the present moment, but to the circumstances that are arising in the present moment. Rather than focusing on the chaotic circumstances in the present moment, place awareness on the quiet underneath the circumstances.

The present moment is not to be confused with bloody noses, angry people, stained floors, or conference calls. It is only right now, which is always peaceful. It is the quiet backdrop underneath whatever circumstances are unfolding, but it is not the circumstances themselves.

To take this one step deeper, the present moment is the same thing as *you.*

Because this is a strange idea for most people to grasp—that a "no-thing" can be compared to an apparent live being such as a person—it will be touched upon several different times. Since the stillness that inherently resides in the present moment is the precise stillness that inherently resides with *you,* it can be said that the present moment and you are synonymous.

The environment can be very noisy and chaotic, but a conscious person would still be able to detect presence underneath the ruckus, and *that* is to what they are consciously anchored. When you can detect stillness, and can recognize that stillness as *yourself,* you are awakening. This is why the term is referred to as "self-realization."

The internal equivalent of a loud noisy room is loud, constant, inner mental chatter. That is why the opposite of pure presence or pure consciousness is compulsive mental thought.

*When the still, inner essence is uncovered from its oppressor— egoic mental noise—presence begins to more frequently align with itself: the present moment. This alignment virtually guarantees inner peace and a chronic state of well-being, no matter the outer circumstances.*

This idea, that your true essence is virtually identical to the "now" is impossible for the mind to comprehend, so if you're having trouble understanding this, it's not surprising. Instead, allow your essence to *feel* the truth of it. The mind cannot comprehend that which is its opposite. It only knows about matter and form. Since language and the use of words that comprise it are also matter, it is difficult to describe that which is *not* matter, using a vehicle (language, words) that *is* matter. This is why all ancient spiritual texts tell of the impossibility of speaking about divine ideas. It is why the incomprehensible Zen Koan is meant to stop the mind so you can go beyond it. One can attempt it as we are doing here, but the use of words always presents an imprecise application. How can you use a word to describe "no-thing"? It's like trying to use a word to describe a color to a blind person who has never had sight. Pure consciousness is the same as life essence; it is the same as presence, but it is not a *thing*. It is an invisible force, yet is difficult to describe, so the mind objects that it doesn't understand. Simply be aware of this mental objection and allow yourself to feel the truth of it anyway. The mind is a tool and because it cannot understand concepts having to do with that which sources it, it rejects it out of hand, even though your acceptance of and alignment with the present moment is the only guarantee of peace.

Your inner essence, the life that sustains you, is made up of pure space. It is invisible. It is the opposite of matter and in fact, is what *animates* matter. That's why the mind has no idea what this discussion is about. You can't expect that a teenager can run NASA. Well, you can, but you won't get good results. Although we have believed that the mind is the premier conductor of life, this is incorrect. It is merely a tool. So how can a tool be expected to comprehend ideas that have to do with the source that created it? It can't. That's why understanding this concept is not necessary to begin effective spiritual practice. The practice itself will begin to dissolve the obstacle to understanding, and paradoxically, once the process of dissolving the egoic mind structure begins, more awareness is recaptured, which in turn enables you to recognize just how "demonic" your previous captor really was. Finally, the tool that had once grown into a beast is no longer running the show.

*Presence that animates the tool of the mind is the only appropriate "manager" of life because presence is exactly the same as life. Finally, we are allowing life to be in charge, rather than the mind, a counterfeit replica.*

When life is allowed to *be,* without the loud, chronic resistance of the mind, it's extraordinary how problems mysteriously smooth out and relationships are healed. The reason why this occurs is that life's presence is inherently peaceful and lovely in its simplicity and is thus predictably soothing and is the perfect healer of you and others.

When you are able to stay magically peaceful no matter the outer circumstances, you are aligned with the present moment. Because you are no longer resisting the present, you are able to become more of what you already are. In this way, presence's power becomes fully charged because it's finally uncovered from all that compulsively loud mental chatter. The servant has been demoted and peace is now in charge. When you are calm and at peace despite outer chaos, you are aligned with the present moment. The "now" is constant in its stillness and perfection. It is the animating presence *underneath* whatever is happening.

You have now touched your own power. As lovely and as celebratory as is the reinstatement of presence's power, the mind as tyrant won't relinquish the throne easily. Any attempt to *remain* at peace is initially met with alarming mental reaction. The cunning aspect of the analytical mind recognizes its impending dissolution and becomes triggered into extreme survival instincts. This takes the form of redoubling its effort in being offended by that which is now threatening it: the actual process of properly identifying it through description, definition, and examples of its cunning agenda, and effective spiritual practice. That's why the egoic mind wants you dead. As stated previously, at the very least, it's constantly on guard, looking for ways to keep *you* from noticing *it*. Can you catch how this agenda is alive within you, even as you react to what you are reading here?

We have already discussed the fact that the egoic mind likes to be active, noisy, figuring things out, and making a complexity out of nothing. A noisy mind stands in the way of spiritual growth.

The minds of the Alzheimer's patient and that of any DP or child who is in a temper tantrum are the perfect noisy minds. Because the busy mind doesn't want to be found out, it does its compulsive figuring and analyzing, all in the name of trying to "simplify" things or trying to "make things better." It tries to cover up its real goal of creating havoc. The mind loves to get its hands into problems and improve upon them. Although it calls this sort of noisy mind "helping," it is really a disguised form of killing the quiet self within. Of course, your inner essence cannot really be killed; however, it can be almost entirely obscured.

The Alzheimer's mind, due to its impairment, has simplified this chronic state of mental chaos by simply resisting most everything carte blanche. It also becomes more and more fixated on cleaning, fixing, or straightening things in the world of form, but does so in a simplified way in its environment. At first glance it looks as though the patient is happily puttering or wandering. In reality, the mouth may be silent, but the noisy mind still drives the person with a whip as demonstrated by their almost complete inability to be still and do nothing. If the patient is, out of necessity, "forced" to do nothing, then the mind will figure out some other way in which to keep the habit going in objecting to this thing or that. This characteristic is shared by the DP, as well as most normal people and busy teenagers and children.

For example, Jeannette and I were sitting in the waiting room of her doctor's office when a woman in her mid-fifties entered the room. Jeannette, consistent with her lifelong judgment of others' appearance, accidentally said loudly enough for the other woman to hear, "Now *there's* a facelift gone wrong!"

As was customary in such situations, I apologized for Jeannette's comment and privately told the woman that she has Alzheimer's. "Ah yes," she responded knowingly and proceeded to tell me of her own experience with a dementia patient in her family. Frequently, others who learn of Jeannette's illness are eager to share "horror stories" about the difficulties in caring for a DP. They always include a description of the degree and intensity behind the patient's intolerance of everything. Upon observing any DP, the student of spirituality can see how their own mind stays equally troubled and frequently condemns whatever it experiences.

In the example of the waiting room, Jeannette was at ease and comfortable; however, it took only two minutes for her dysfunctional mind to identify something to which it could object. The mind's degree of dysfunction knows no limits. This is not surprising, given what we already know about the DP: they create havoc and suffering for themselves and others in their environment, *unless* . . . that person is a courageous seeker who wishes to grow spiritually and is capable of conceiving of their own deficits by using the DP as a mirror.

It is a common habit for almost everyone, not just those with Alzheimer's, to secretly critique others. Until the mind is stilled, this is a dysfunctional habit that involves condemning others in order to feel superior, all under the guise of "people watching." But are you really watching when you do this? True "people watching" involves *watching* without mental commentary. But the mind stays busy and focused on meaninglessness and minutia. It is restless, searching, and chronically acting out its unsettled chaos, until you, the inner being, reinstate proper authority.

The dementia patient's mind and that of the DP are angry at little things. Their mind rejects out of hand the simplest circumstance, which places itself in a chronic state of moral superiority to almost everyone and every circumstance with which it comes into contact. This mindset is only a slightly exaggerated version of our own.

Aligning with negativity by focusing on it keeps the mind agitated by comparing and contrasting itself with others. This is how it regenerates itself.

*The noisy mind feeds on negative energy and must have moment-to-moment feedings to ensure its survival.*

The mind is not you; it is an overlay, which, through thousands of years of evolution, has grown into a near-entity with false importance and negative influence, like a school bully who evolved into a dictator. This is the reason for social and environmental decline.

As we have discussed, most people have assumed that the mind is the same as *you.* This is a common error, but you are not the mind. You are not your thoughts. You, as pure essence, are life itself. You cannot be changed or destroyed, although the mind and the body can be. The mind wreaks havoc by taking you over. It has done a marvelous job of this because almost everyone believes that their very thoughts are them, and worse, that by virtue of having a thought, it must be true.

Effective spiritual practice to lessen the grip of your mind's hold on you involves lessening the dominant role of the analytical mind. The mind can be used as a tool, but as in the case of the Alzheimer's patient and the DP, the tool has taken the being over almost entirely and is now routing all perceptions through its dysfunctional screen. This is why when you finally put into place effective spiritual practices that enable you to calm down for a change, the mind goes on alert status and wants to reestablish its control. It cannot tolerate cooperating with practices that are certain to lessen, or even substantially dissolve, its own domain.

Quieting the mind is not the same as having *no* mind. The quiet mind has simply been placed in its proper hierarchy. It becomes a tool, rather than the master. It is used, rather than allowing it to use *you*, which can come as a shock if all this time you thought you *were* your mind and that your thoughts and opinions that arise are gospel.

You are an immortal being of pure essence which *has* a mind that can be used as a tool for working at a profession, planning a trip, or running a household. But even in these cases, as will be discussed later, thinking must be interspersed with moments of "space" or "presence" in order to remain at peace and to grow spiritually. Further, the most efficient, powerful, and clear creativity always arises out of a quiet mind. Most people believe that the mind itself is doing the creating, but this is not accurate. The mind is used to funnel the creativity into a practical means, but the creative force itself is never borne from mind activity. The essence of you, the presence of you itself *uses* the mind, or, at least this is the proper order once mind's activity has quieted. In addition, thought, surrounded by periods of quiet, ensure that what *is* derived from thought is the most effective and creative solution possible.

In and of itself, the mind is useful. The trouble arises because the mind has gotten out of control, and is now running the entire show. The being is so subservient to it that, even the suggestion that the mind's thoughts are not true, provokes disbelief. It is painfully obvious only when you have the benefit of observing the mind of the Alzheimer's patient, which can believe the most extraordinary falsehoods and hold them as truth. The patient may believe that their personal articles are in constant danger of being stolen. Those who have very busy and active minds, like the Alzheimer's patient, may hoard and covet every trinket, viewing the changing economy or other people as a threat to its stash. The patient may at times complain that lunch was never eaten, even when a caregiver points to the plate of food, now mostly gone. Anyone who attempts to refute a so-called truth held by the patient is met with abject annoyance or even fury.

This is also the normal state of consciousness (prior to enlightenment) wherein we also believe that the thoughts that pop into our mind are true and must be negatively reacted to, and believed, and then acted upon. This includes any thought that produces suffering. Of course, some thoughts that indicate danger may indeed be accurate; however, simple action can be taken without need of mental commentary and a story about how awful life is. But 99 percent of all thought tends to be negative, worrisome, and critical, and is by its nature false, or not true. Imagine then how people, in a preawakened state, exist when the majority of the thoughts that pop into their mind are not even true. Now, you are finally getting a glimpse into the actual dismal condition of the mind and how it sponsors most people's actions.

Feelings that *appear* to be thoughts, ones that have to do with love, beauty, appreciation, gratitude, compassion, etc., are not thoughts at all, but are an outpouring from within you as pure consciousness. Life is expressing itself through you as these feelings, but technically, they are not thoughts at all, nor can they be borne from a mind that is necessarily noisy by nature. Or, the opposite: thoughts disguised as feelings like thoughts of love, where we are wanting or needing something from someone. Obviously, real love needs or wants nothing from anyone in order to feel satisfied or complete.

The determining factor between thoughts that produce suffering, and ideas that inspire and encourage, is that the former are manufactured by the egoic thought structure and are not actually true; the latter *flow through you* as sourced by life. If you take notice of the cause the next time you feel sad, afraid, and angry or stressed, you will find a thought (that is not true) believed to be true. Strictly speaking, feelings and ideas that do not produce suffering are not created by the mind.

This distinction is helpful so that you will know which feelings to believe and which to know are a lie. Because the analytical mind exists to keep you in denial of your alignment with the true powerful essence of you, it comes up with chronic, counterfeit thoughts that keep you consistently reacting and responding to an environment that it says is unsafe. The analytical mind loves nothing more than stirring up trouble within interpersonal relationships and looks for any excuse to take offense. Any thought that causes worry or upset is borne from a noisy mind. Any feeling that inspires or feels love is borne from stillness, from the power of pure stillness in the present moment, and is not, by definition, a thought. Making a careful distinction between these two engenders a desire to end the cause of suffering by quieting a noisy mind.

You can still use the mind's thoughts to recognize danger and quickly flee; however, you are doing so in a state of calm presence without drama and mental objection. You clearly assess what is needed in the moment and carry that action through. There is no complaining and objecting, no angry commentary and reaction that "this shouldn't be happening," and particularly, there is no fear or upset that you have been wronged or misused. Since suggesting that you can accept the present moment, but still make changes, seems very foreign, I later include a practice that can assist in dissolving compulsive thought which inherently causes discomfort and problems.

Any spiritual practice that does not include an effective way to dissolve the egoic mind will not be very effective. Most practices *can't* dissolve it because they *use* the mind in the practice. For example, Eckhart Tolle uses the analogy of a chief of police who is trying to locate and arrest the arsonist, when the chief *is* the arsonist.

Since enlightenment means the end of the egoic mind, the analytical mind will never orchestrate its own undoing, which is why it finds fault with simple and effective practices that actually work, or with the very words that define it. Imagine how the chief of police would predictably find fault with an independent investigator, or the practices, procedures, or vocabulary used to conduct the investigation. He wouldn't be able to tolerate any effective practice or means of identifying the villain (including words used to define what the villain's characteristics are) that would make a break in the case.

If you want to observe a perfect example of the analytical mind in all its cunning and destructive glory, simply observe the addictive voice of any alcoholic or addict. This voice (the mind which is addicted to chaos and problems) is that inner urging that takes over the alcoholic or addict and pretends to be him and gets the person to act on its behalf. The addictive voice will use any means possible to get the addict to inject, imbibe, or ingest certain substances, to its own detriment. It lives to get poison into the bloodstream. The addict's addictive voice, which urges the person to drink or use, has no mercy whatsoever and cares nothing of the destruction and chaos that it initiates, even if the outcome is intense emotional and physical suffering and death. The addict's voice is only a slightly exaggerated version of the "normal," everyday, garden-variety analytical mind that is also addicted and in constant need of a virtual daily "fix" of worry and negativity. It is cunning, virtually hell-bent on destruction, and will not rest until the inner essence of the being is completely obscured by mental suffering.

When the addict or alcoholic, who attempts to remain clean and sober, is almost seduced by their inner addictive voice but is at least able to recognize that this voice is not them, which in turn empowers the refusal to capitulate to its demands, they are finally on the way to abstinence and sanity. Indeed, effective abstinence *begins* with the no-holds-barred approach to first identifying the nature and characteristics of the addictive voice. Without recognizing the way that it seduces one, with a line of thinking that seeks alcohol or substance abuse, the addict cannot recover. Alas, even during recovery, mental objections that deny a need for abstinence is the addictive voice itself. Indeed, addicts and alcoholics require complete abstinence for a full recovery. There are no half-measures. Any attempt to use moderately is in itself evidence that an addiction still exists. Recovered addicts learn to recognize the strong pull of that deep unconscious pleasure that provides an instant rush when they drink or use drugs. Despite the stated goals of many long-term recovery programs, an instantaneous recognition of the nature of the addictive voice can bring immediate sobriety and no further adherence to any program is needed. Once you recognize the inner addict's voice (whether to problems, alcohol, or drugs), you can immediately effect your own instantaneous recovery without further need of expensive, extensive, or long-standing therapies or solutions. As such, any voice that seduces using substances to attain this deep pleasure or release can be accurately classified as the addictive voice. That is how the addict begins to recognize that this voice is not them, since they know that drinking or using causes untold destruction and no amount of momentary unconscious pleasure can create peace or happiness. This is how effective substance abuse recovery occurs.

Analogously, the student of spirituality is also on a path of recovery and recognizes the addictive voice of the analytical mind. The seeker learns that its own addictive voice doesn't want to be found out, so it—the analytical mind—denies that its voice is deadly. The seeker learns to identify compulsive thought that is chronically angry or annoyed—or the way that it denies the voracity of its addiction—as threatening its sober peace. In the same way that the addictive voice lives to get poison into the bloodstream, the analytical mind exists to get negative thoughts into the awareness of the spiritual practitioner. Without having identified the addictive voice, the seeker will not recognize its inroads on a precious, yet possibly still tenuous, state of inner calm. But the analytical mind will object to the very idea that its purpose is vicious and cunning, and it will attempt to keep alive the addiction to the deep unconscious pleasure of reacting negatively. Just as the recovered addict clearly recognizes an inner urging to drink or use as the addictive voice and not as him, the seeker too can immediately recognize any thought as ill sponsored if it causes fear, annoyance, objection, upset, or stress. Indeed, once you can truly face, without flinching, the characteristic of that which steals your peace or attempts to take over your true essence, you are almost all the way there. However, the seeker, unlike the recovered addict, may not yet have recognized its own desire for the deep unconscious pleasure that is attained from focusing on problems or meaningless minutia. Like the addictive voice that needs a fix, the analytical mind needs and feeds on drama and ideas of instability to sustain it. It is addicted to the deep unconscious pleasure of mental suffering.

To clarify, you still use the mind just fine for practical purposes once your awakening is underway. You can plan for the future, but such planning is not done compulsively in a way that creates mental suffering and worry. *The mind is picked up as a tool and then put down.* It does not run rampant over stillness and peace, the only true source of lasting serenity. And here lies the crux of the challenge:

*If the egoic mind is an entity of sorts that wants to survive, then dethroning it entails certain challenges that have not been historically overcome in large numbers of people. It cannot be stated enough: the mind will never orchestrate its own undoing despite the fact that the process to full awakening is straightforward. The mind is very clever and is astute for evidence of attack.*

In order to awaken spiritually, you must become friendly with the present moment. Surrender to what *is*. This is the counterpoint to the mind's demand for negative emotional reactions to never-ending minutia. Changes can still be made, but such changes are made while in the surrendered state of equanimity. This act of surrendering prior to attempting to make changes or impart correction increases the energy field and vibration of the physical body. This heightened energy field can actually be felt by sensitive individuals standing nearby. The higher and faster the body's energy field, the more resistant it is to illness and "contagious" negative moods of others. In addition, higher energy fields are pleasurable to be around, although most people would not be able to discern the reason for their attraction. Awakened individuals are often construed as likeable. They are simpler than most people because they have no false identity to uphold and thus are not seeking an advantage, or staving off misfortune.

To awaken, become more aligned with consciousness, and less aligned with chronic thought. This is adding that which is the opposite of a noisy mind: increased quietness and spaciousness around your everyday events. This does not mean that you need to be in a quiet room or to live in the middle of a forest. It means that within the business of life, you add consciousness by quieting the mind, even if the environment remains noisy. The spiritual practice that makes this possible is easier than meditation and is extremely simple to put into place. (There is a specific practice that can be used for this which is described in detail in chapter 5.) Through this process, the entire egoic mind structure begins to dissolve. From that point on, thought cannot hold you hostage to ideas that would normally create suffering. You realize your true identity as life itself and no longer fret and focus on minutia.

Once awakened, it is as though you are waking up from a deep troubled sleep where nightmares had occurred on a regular basis. Now you know why there have been reports from ancient times of people experiencing overwhelming joy and relief when entering the enlightened state. From that point on, no problem can present itself, because all "things"—bodies, cars, thoughts, buildings, careers, etc., are all recognized as unstable and ever changing, so the awakened individual does not get trapped in a permanent illusion that form should be anything *but* that. The awakened person can still enjoy all that is of form, including bodily sensations and the ease of a life with comforts; however, they are not needed to sustain well-being. "Luxuries" are simply enjoyed while available, and if not available due to any reason at all, that's okay too.

Sadness, tears, or anger can still be felt or expressed, but they occur on the surface, like a ripple on the ocean; they no longer run deep, nor do they take up residence for any length of time. The awakened person is grounded in consciousness: her/his essence is identified with life, instead of form and false identities. This is the grace that arises in allowing the river of life to take its own course. The present moment is allowed to *be*. Once accepted and surrendered to, changes or corrections can always be made, but resistance is no longer the normal way of reacting to other people and events.

When you adopt an effective spiritual practice, until full enlightenment has been attained, you go back and forth between these states of being. It can feel so drastic at times it's as if you are actually moving between two entirely different worlds. But enlightenment means that you exist solely in the new world where peace reigns and you operate from that perspective. But until then, you will waffle. This is the new paradigm for awakening wherein the seeker moves in and out of full awareness, becoming more and more attuned to the analytical mind's attempt to seduce you into seeking out or creating everyday problematic events and experiences for the deep unconscious pleasure they provide.

Be cognizant that you are awakening amidst a full-blown cultural hypnosis. Almost none of the general population knows what enlightenment actually is, let alone supports you in your practice to uncover it. Few recognize the incredible way that the quality of life can shift for the better. Instead, the collective mind structure has trained the world's population to find solace in demonstrating a cunning and clever mind by identifying, focusing upon, and trying to solve minutia. In addition, the national pastime continues to be accumulating things and achieving status and respect. Naturally, peace and happiness can never be found in this way, evidenced by those who have keen minds, superb intellects, and/or wealth and respect and are still miserable. A profound example of this is when an Alzheimer's patient who is well cared for and surrounded by others who love her will pathologically, albeit unconsciously, seek out the one irritant that can be reacted against.

Even among spiritual seekers, there is misunderstanding as to what this powerful shift of awakening entails. Many assume that enlightenment is simply "living by the golden rule" and squeezing in an hour of daily meditation. This misunderstanding is akin to describing Niagara Falls as something "wet." This explanation doesn't get close to describing this state by several orders of magnitude, and so you miss the essence and very definition entirely. In addition, you miss the invitation to fully participate in awakening yourself. If you think you already have what it is, then you have no reason to participate in the process. If you think enlightenment is simply living an ethical life without drama, that's not it.

Enlightenment represents the most extraordinary shift in human evolution. It is the single most significant shift since the first living cells became multi-cell organisms. It is the Nirvana promised by so many religious practices, although early scribes often misunderstood it as a desireless almost inanimate state, when it is the fruition of human potential at all levels.

Imagine the people on Earth before and after a huge shift in spiritual consciousness: Pre-enlightenment, the cultural bias for individuals and institutions serves the egoic mind structure. There is compulsive critiquing, comparing, judging, assessing, with a tendency to regret past mistakes and to worry about future ones; compulsive planning to avoid loss of status, health, wealth, or relationships, and last but not least, accumulation of stuff, or strategies to get it from those who have it. This is considered normal.

When we think about improving our world, we think about ridding ourselves of terrorists and drug lords and wars. We rarely notice just how much suffering each person creates for themselves, their partner, children, family, work environments, and society, even when a person is considered by most standards to be rather high-functioning and "responsible."

The standard for success in normal culture doesn't even address a peaceful state of mind as a worthy "achievement," or even of any value. A dysfunctional culture doesn't believe that chronic serenity is necessary, or even possible.

In a spiritual tradition, the person who is deemed as the most "successful," whether in a monastery or out in the world, is the one who has achieved the quietest mind, which in turn produces the highest quality of being because no suffering is created for yourself or others. It's the ultimate, "the buck stops here" approach to world peace. First, stop the insanity within yourself, and you'll be amazed at how much peace is created in the community around you, your home, and your work environment.

Human minds that are not yet awakened differ only in their degree of noisiness and compulsivity. Some minds are so noisy and compulsive, so dysfunctional and destructive, that they drive their human host to suicide. Other minds, although not depressed or suicidal, may still be viciously noisy. These people are said to be "difficult." They are said to be a perfectionist or hard on others. Translation: their mind savages others through their chronic faultfinding and habitual correcting of them and generally creates suffering in most any environment.

Most of our minds are somewhere in the middle and do a fair amount of condemnation of everyone and most every situation with which they come into contact. Most people go back and forth between a shallow happiness when something wanted is purchased, or a goal is achieved or gained; and "unhappiness," when their mind objects to something or someone, or objects to the way and manner that the present moment *is*, and they can't "fix" it.

Because the mind feeds on negative thoughts, it compulsively focuses on the future, or rewinds mental tapes of past offenses. Usually the exception is when witnessing the intense beauty in nature, experiencing deep love, or when death appears imminent. In these cases the mind slows or stops momentarily. But soon after, it starts back up again, chronically complaining about the weather, traffic, political scene, pollution, body weight, another's behavior, etc. This is the normal state of human consciousness or the lack thereof.

The egoic mind is excruciatingly cunning. It has become so evolved and over eons so intertwined with so-called human development that it's normal to believe that you *are* your mind. This is the crux of the challenge before us.

*To deal with an entity whose cunning knows no superior, takes an extraordinary level of courage because the very practice that dissolves its reign will be the very one to which your own mind will object.*

This is the nature of the work set out before any serious student of spirituality.

*Attaining enlightenment, or at least an awakening, involves the sustaining of an ultimate paradox. Alas, the heart of effective spiritual practice involves continuously getting beyond the mind's objections to actually behold the unsavory characteristics of the insidious analytical mind, and to the practice itself that dissolves it.*

The analytical mind's most common objection to effective spiritual practice can be easily predicted. Since the mind thrives on and adores complexity, it shuns simplicity. The mind seeks busyness. It fears stillness. When you begin a practice to quiet the mind, it will protest in extraordinary ways. First, it will convince you that no aspect of your analytical mind wants you dead; that you don't really have such a cunning and deceptive inner beast, as is the case with the addict's addictive voice. Second, it will try to convince you that it doesn't have time for spiritual practice, or that it isn't really needed, wanted, or necessary. Instead, the mind wants you to focus on its "problems"—the very problems that it alone has created and then identifies as important and needing attention. Third, it will attempt to make a new enemy out of any simple effective spiritual practice. To the contrary, the analytical mind loves programs that are complicated and expensive and that require a lot of mental computations while promising spiritual improvement. Simpler programs, which beautifully allow the inner being to clearly recognize and thus dissolve their addictive voice (analytical mind) that yearns for drama and chaos, are predictably shunned.

The single most effective spiritual practice when applied daily is to simplify your life and be quiet. Yet the mind says "No!" we're not doing this now. The mind will attempt to divert you. It says, "Look over there. That's a problem that needs to be taken care of." The mind doesn't like spiritual practice that quiets its compulsivity. It will insist that it has more important things to do. It will remind you, again and again, particularly in the midst of your attempt to quiet it, that there's an important problem that can't be ignored. This is how it gets its way over and over again, until you become aware of just how much deep unconscious pleasure has been attained by using these destructive strategies.

The enlightened being responds to the mind, "No, I'm looking at *you*. I'm looking at how you attempt to operate in me."

Unfortunately, this practice becomes impossible for the Alzheimer's patient as they progress further into the disease; however, everyone else is capable of making this detachment. Yet even the dementia patient benefits from those around her, when they refuse to follow her egoic dictates and negative compulsivity, which only seems to temporarily quiet the mind.

When the patient or any DP consistently throws up an objection to one problem after another, notice the mechanics of it. Notice how this noisy mind can only stay unperturbed for just so long before it gleefully finds something or someone to which it can loudly object. If nothing is available to which it *can* object, it will make something up. Observe this pattern in another and you will see that this is the case. Then, you will undoubtedly notice a similar pattern within yourself. Notice another's deep unconscious pleasure while in the midst of drama, and then you may notice your own.

Spiritual seekers or family and caregivers of a DP must hold fast to the truth of life: that somehow there is perfection, even within a context of apparent difficulty, although it's hard to understand. To agree with the Alzheimer's mind or the mind of any DP that all is lost, and that mental suffering over trivialities is normal, is to feed and thus enhance the mind's ability to create suffering for the beloved patient and those around them.

*Only by dissolving the egoic structure through your own example can there be any degree of peace and calm in a household or community, whether or not Alzheimer's is present.*

And so the average person's entire life is spent going from one thing to another, attempting to fix problems with which the mind chronically identifies. Instead, if an alignment with the present is added daily, problems tend to right themselves; or, if action or correction needs to be taken, action becomes efficient, clear, and effective. Such action is of an entirely different order than the action arising from discontent and an upset mind. Important decisions easily make themselves. Timely right action can be determined and put into place.

But the mind doesn't want transformation because it recognizes rightly that its domain becomes diminished as transformation arises. Thus, you, the diligent student of spirituality must train yourself to observe the ways and means that your mind disqualifies effective spiritual practice as soon as it starts.

Despite its incredible simplicity, this is why truly effective spiritual practice is so rarely applied, even though it produces immediate results in the short term and powerfully transformative results in the long term. What the analytical mind doesn't know is that an altogether different order of deep pleasure is available from a secure alignment with inner peace. This is a *conscious* deep pleasure and is permanent, and so unlike the counterfeit pleasure sponsored by the analytical mind, it is of course not unconscious and so does not create secondary problems.

This alignment with peace is the urge toward wholeness and cannot be long ignored from an evolutionary standpoint. If you hear the call, it is easily heeded. It beckons you to a deeper level of existence, wherein your relationships and environment become transformed by nothing more than your own example of serenity. Once you discover where your true nourishment lies, you will naturally begin to align with it on an ever-increasing basis.

Something lovely is emerging from the depths. It is you, your true nature, ready and willing to be uncovered, long obscured by the analytical mind's ploys. Although it may feel as though you are now leaping empty handed into the void of the unknown, trust the river of life to carry you to your new life as a bearer of peace. Your family and all who know you will be deeply blessed by your example.

# 4

The Emotional Pain Body

IN HIS SEMINAL BOOK, *The Power of Now,* spiritual teacher Eckhart Tolle describes the nature of what he calls, the "emotional pain body." As part of the egoic mind structure, there is a heavy, dense, negative energy field attached to a human being's body and mind, which operates as though it were an entity in and of itself and can take over and control us. Eckhart describes it as a "true demon."

This extremely dense, negative energy creates our emotional reactions and stores them as emotional memories that become a history of sort, which can then trigger further outbursts of a similar nature. It grows during times of stress, illness, a death in the family, or loss and is triggered by something that the mind says has "gone wrong." Most people characterize a true pain body's active state as a bad mood or temper tantrum. It is present in chronic patterns, emerging predictably on a daily, weekly, or monthly basis. It sits there lurking just under the surface to strike out at any given opportunity the mind finds.

When the pain body suddenly takes over a person, anyone can recognize it. This is when a person becomes mean-spirited, revoltingly self-centered, sharply critical, and generally just horrible to be around. In late-stage Alzheimer's disease, the patient has become almost entirely taken over by the pain body, as is no doubt the case in many textbook psychiatric disorders. Any DP can also be said to have a very dense and active pain body.

The pain body, like the mind of which it is part, wants to survive at any cost to you. You will know that it is active in yourself or others when you see intense displays of anger, rage, irritation, jealousy, self-righteous condemnation, tearfulness, sadness, or bitter faultfinding. Any chronic emotional reactivity can be traced to an active pain body.

As was mentioned earlier, Jeannette was in chronic negative resistance to the feeding tube that had been inserted at her abdomen, although it was established that there was virtually no physical discomfort inherent in the feeding process. She would erupt into loud wailing and physical resistance whenever I would attempt to insert a syringe of Ensure. In addition, she needed to be monitored at every moment because she became fixated on the idea of emptying the contents, which of course was her food and bile and all the liquid contents of her stomach. For many months, she tried getting to a toilet, sometimes every ten minutes, so that she could empty it. After locks were installed on the bathroom doors, she would pound on the doors in fury. Despite frequent bathroom breaks, she turned the household upside down in a game of cat and mouse over her feeding tube. At one point, it became necessary to simply place her in a car and drive her up and down the coast for five or six hours a day, simply in order to find an environment in which to contain her. Together, we put a lot of miles on the car.

Although it would appear that her strong reaction was natural given her dementia, what was seldom recognized by others is that, if she were not fighting and reacting to her G-tube, she would have simply found another "reason" to stay unhappy, complaining and holding her environment hostage to her temper tantrums. It is Jeannette's very dense and active pain body, not her Alzheimer's, that emerges frequently to "feed" on negativity. This means that, like everyone's, her pain body actually *needs* a problem on which to react and thus feed. Predictably, because her pain body was habituated all her life to create havoc through her emotional outbursts, disapproval, and chronic complaining, her feeding tube was just another opportunity.

For most of her life, Jeannette demonstrated a very strong personality and became easily aroused to displeasure or anger. Her sister tells the story of how their father picked a nickname for Jeannette, calling her "JoJo, the tiger kid" because she was so feisty and fiery. Instead of having positive attributes, an active pain body is usually moody, angry, and volatile. Some dense pain bodies are destructive beyond measure because they seek to draw everyone or anyone into chronic battles. You can imagine how little peace and serenity there is in such a household or work environment. This means that, unless and until a DP's pain body—or the pain body of anyone who lives or works with a DP—is dissolved through effective spiritual practice, there will be no end to suffering.

When Jeannette eventually lost much of her finger dexterity, I was finally able to cover the cap of the feeding tube with a tubular bandage which she was unable to remove. Within a day or two, her pain body switched its fixation to the refrigerator to get small containers of yogurt to feed the dog. Keep in mind that the pain body has an unconscious brilliance to some degree. It knows exactly what will elicit a reaction or response from those in the environment. The pain body seeks to engage, and will always be able to find a new reason to fly into a fury. In the case of the family dog, Jeannette had long recognized that Kenya had gained thirty-five pounds and had trouble walking and getting up from a sitting or sleeping position. With arthritis and skin problems, Kenya was on a diet with medication. So now, instead of attempting to empty her feeding tube, which she could no longer do, Jeannette would still retreat to the bathroom, but now to sneak the dog more food. Despite her cognitive declines, she nonetheless was still aware that she was breaking a family rule, because when she would sneak off, she first looked to see if anyone noticed and would always feed the dog yogurt in the privacy of her bedroom or bathroom. So, addicted to drama, the pain body will find any way possible to keep others negatively engaged with it. When I then hid all the yogurt, she switched to yet another tactic to stay chronically engaged: she began to push a tissue or towel down her throat, which caused her to erupt into gagging fits. This behavior replaced the compulsion with her feeding tube and feeding snacks to the dog and effectively served to draw in anyone who was near her . Naturally, she strongly reacted to anyone's attempt to stop this behavior, and so the cycle continued. Although perhaps this is an exaggerated case, can you see this dynamic alive within your DP or your own children?

The insidious nature of the pain body when it becomes activated is that there is virtually no amount of reasoning, cajoling, or begging that can stop it; that is, until it has had its fill and it retreats, satiated . . . until the next time. In addition, because each person's pain body attracts others of a similar makeup, when one person's pain body becomes active, others around them get triggered as well. And then as the saying goes, you're "off to the races."

When the pain body is triggered within you, it will take over your mind, which may already be dysfunctional, and does the thinking for you. It then confuses you by pretending to be you when it is in its active stage. You see this all the time when people get carried away by their emotions and appear to be driven by something. The pain body can do untold damage without remorse and very active ones are responsible for all of the worst examples of human violence.

For most average humans, the pain body gets triggered by outside events every three or four days or perhaps once per week, especially within relationships. The emotional reactions that occur in interpersonal relationships bring it out to feed. It needs to feed to stay alive. Because the pain body is the dark shadow cast by the ego, which is an aspect of the analytical mind, finding fault with others is its hallmark characteristic. Pain bodies feed on negativity, ready to react when the mind finds something which it can object to or improve upon. The extreme example of one gone rampant is the Alzheimer's patient who becomes agitated on a continual basis, with only short periods of respite.

Pain bodies present differently to different people. If you're a depressed person, your pain body has turned on *you*. When it's active, you feel deep sadness, depression, self-doubt, hopelessness, or despair. The person who is verbally or physically abused, as well as their perpetrator, both experience active pain bodies. Although a victim would deny that he or she "needs" the abuse drama, there is an unconscious need for them to feed their pain body, which is why it attracts similar active, abusive pain bodies. Victim and perpetrator match pain bodies and unconsciously seek each other out in order to feed. They unconsciously, but very effectively, use each other to provide the needed negative drama and its energy. This feeding occurs as love relationships are formed and even when two strangers get in an argument or meet in a traffic accident.

Few recognize that daily drama is actually *needed* by the pain body, and it is cunning in the way that it will ensure pulling drama out of ordinary, everyday neutral circumstances. The Alzheimer's patient has been taken over by the pain body to the degree that it becomes difficult to help them dis-identify from it. In late-stage Alzheimer's, it may be in a chronically active state and unconsciously exists to feed itself. Almost every waking moment is spent in service to it. Consciously adding stillness and presence is the family's and caregiver's only hope for their own sanity. They must be consciously on the alert for the pain body's emergence, and become rooted in their own stillness in order to prevent theirs from becoming activated. Anyone who undergoes dramatic but consistent mood swings is experiencing the cycles of an active and dormant pain body. This is also the case for anyone who is in a frequent state of mental suffering, Alzheimer's diagnosis or not.

Women can recognize the pain body as that "overly sensitive" and critical, dense emotional and physical energy that emerges several days prior to the onset of menstruation. Many women's pain bodies also become activated during hormonal changes such as when pregnant. Socially, we have described its onset as a time when a woman is "difficult," or "hormonal." At these times the woman readily objects to what is said or done or whatever is occurring in the present moment. Active pain bodies are all about objecting to what *is*; they are faultfinders extraordinaire, but cannot, while in the active stage, recognize their own tendency to objection—that is until one matures spiritually and the process of awakening is underway.

Men's and women's pain bodies can be quickly activated when alcohol or other substances are ingested and are responsible for the extreme mood shifts seen in users. Virtually all abuse, both verbal and physical, occurs when a perpetrator's pain body is in an active state.

Some spiritual seekers have dissolved much of their pain

body through integrative practices without realizing it, although they may wonder why they are still not fully awakened. In this case, adding the final touches of presence's power will shrink it to nothing.

If your pain body is very intense, don't be discouraged. Sometimes, the more active and dense it is, the more motivated you are to awaken to ease the pain of suffering. This occurs in the same way that a sleeping person is more likely to spontaneously awaken from a nightmare but not from a regular dream. So recognize that your own strong, dense pain body can definitely be a catalyst for enlightenment.

Everyone has experienced a relationship in which they have been shocked to discover, for the first time, that their formerly sweet, gentle beloved has suddenly turned into a monster when his or her pain body becomes activated. This active stage is not a "mood." It is a sudden transformation from angel to apparent demon and demonstrates how the pain body takes over its host so completely.

Alzheimer's disease demonstrates this perfectly in the patient's aggression, rage, and chronic resistance and complaining. When you are able to recognize the exact way in which an Alzheimer's patient's tirade—or any DP's for that matter—mimics your own, although perhaps to a much lesser degree, then you are ready to take the next step and dissolve your pain body.

Many men's active pain bodies turn on themselves, and the person can become sullen, withdrawn, or feel a need to be alone. Watching television provides a common way to feed it, although it is not normally recognized as anything but a harmless waste of time. However, because television shows are often violent, and their attendant commercials contain a constant stream of noisiness, in addition to a virtual chronic flow of negative thought (even when it's funny), television watching is ideal for pain bodies and noisy minds, but not for uncovering presence.

Simply notice how the negative ideas, comments, and dialogue of your favorite television show matches chronic negative thinking. By observing this dynamic, television watching can become a more conscious habit, less of a feeding frenzy for the pain body, until the habit is less needed.

Pain bodies begin to emerge in childhood as the second birthday approaches. You will know it when you see it because, as already discussed, the nature of the egoic mind structure is to angrily state a defiant "No!" to what *is*. A child's pain body then becomes established within the personality until a later time when the child grows up and can begin to consciously deal with it.

Since every adult has a pain body, children cannot help but inherit their parent's pain body as they witness and experience it growing up; however, there is also a wonderful technique that parents can use to help their own children dis-identify from theirs. In order to help your child become more aware of his active pain body, after a "temper tantrum," wait until they are calm and gently question him about the episode. Bring his awareness to the anger that was expressed, and help him to see how the anger seemed to "take him over." The object is to help him to dis-identify from his pain body, to recognize that it is not really him. If you are a spiritually conscious parent, use examples of when he sees your anger is provoked, and point out to him that yours, too, was in the active stage, and you weren't yourself. As a family, you can use presence to begin to dissolve the pain body's ability to disrupt your environment.

An active pain body always causes suffering for the host or for anyone who happens to be nearby—spouses, lovers, children, relatives, coworkers, acquaintances. There is no limit as to who will be the unlucky receptacle for an active pain body's discharge, with the exception of the seeker who is awakening and thus becomes immune. This is how a normally pleasant person can turn nasty so quickly: the pain body has been triggered and has emerged to feed itself. This is when the person unconsciously gets used by the pain body, which seeks out negative situations, events, people, or circumstances in order to feed. Like an addict's craving for its substance "rush," an active pain body also attains deep pleasure when it objects and reacts negatively. Of course, most people would vehemently deny that this is the case. But be assured, there is no deeper pleasure for a pain body than to disrupt, engage, and create turmoil. This may explain the high divorce rate when considering that everyone has an active pain body, and we unconsciously attract those that trigger ours.

Because the pain body exists in chronic fear of being discovered, its perpetual state is one of fear and defensiveness. This is why a classic narcissist has such a strong dense pain body: it needs to keep itself inflated through attention and flattery to feed its own egoic reflection. Deeply insecure, the pain body is categorically incapable of love, and so fixates its counterfeit love on finding ways to stand out or get approval or flattery. When someone has a very dense pain body that is frequently active, all behaviors exist to enhance its egoic reflection. The pain body is actually a coward in the extreme, in the same way that any mean school bully or perpetrator of abuse often is. Underneath all that bravado is a shallow near-demon, holding on desperately to counterfeit strength and seeking ways to divide and conquer. Quoting Mohandas Gandhi: "A coward is incapable of exhibiting love; it is the prerogative of the brave." Of course, after the pain body has successfully fed itself, it will eventually retreat and your loved one will return all smiles and soft giggles, until its next opportunity.

It's easy to spot an active pain body when it presents itself in extreme, unreasonable ways as is the case of a late-stage

Alzheimer's patient; however, it is very instructive to recognize how it emerges within the context of more socially acceptable circumstances. The pain body is active within everyone, including teenagers and children, and loves to draw egoic attention to itself in an effort to feel morally superior. Culturally, especially in the United States, where a strong, defiant, and even impatient personality is considered a sign of intelligence and character and of "taking charge" of one's environment, we often applaud a pain's body's faultfinding characteristics. It is common for those who consider themselves to be psychologically and emotionally healthy to "call you out" and "confront" inconsistencies or character flaws when observed in another; however, no lasting healing is ever achieved through such tactics. What is achieved, however, is a boost in the pain body's egoic reflection and the deep pleasure it attains when inflating itself.

*Spiritual practice often begins when you are able to observe the nature of the mind and pain body in others; however, true spiritual transformation occurs when you observe your own noisy mind and pain body, rather than judging someone else's. It is good to notice another's pain body as long as you begin to notice your own.*

Because the pain body can only feed on negativity to strengthen itself, in order to awaken spiritually it is this very pain body that is targeted for dissolving. It is when it is mostly dissolved and the normally compulsive and noisy human mind is quieted that a being is said to be enlightened.

Such a person is characterized by a still, quiet mind that accepts the moment as it is. From stillness, breathtaking creativity emerges, or nothing at all. If something needs to be changed or corrected, the enlightened person can do so, but action comes after peaceful acceptance, not before it. There is nothing left of the pain body's resistance. The self-realized person has opinions or preferences but has no cherished ones. With no false ego to uphold, an awakened person is simpler than an ego-driven one and would not stand out as special. Yet the enlightened person is the only being who is truly capable of maintaining long-term love relationships without drama and problems, because unconditional love is the natural outpouring of this new state of consciousness. It's easy to be around someone who is becalmed.

An awakened person can be said to be fully aligned with the essence of life as opposed to the form or matter of life. An enlightened person has become fully aligned with his or her powerful source and knows peace and serenity to a degree that can only be imagined by a non-awakened person. When suffering is absent, peace reigns.

To maintain this seemingly impossible state of ever-present peace, you need only uncover the peace that is already there, but has been obscured by all the noise. This is the heart of effective spiritual practice.

When you are ready, willing, and able to apply effective spiritual practice as a means to uncovering unshakeable serenity, by dissolving the pain body and quieting the mind, you have finally matured, spiritually. Until this point, you are like the Alzheimer's patient or any DP, constantly reacting emotionally to life, compulsively pushing the river, with no hope for lasting peace.

Now that you recognize the obstacle to peace that can be dissolved through effective spiritual practice, let's move on to what that practice entails.

# 5

---

# The Antidote

INTERPERSONAL CONFLICTS WITH COUPLES, or any type of interpersonal relationships, are extremely disheartening because each of us yearns for harmony. We fall in love and then the pain-body dance begins, and we're sick at heart by how our previous tender and supportive union suddenly collapses. When the pain body is active and feeding, there is an unconscious need to negatively engage with the other person—whether the other person is your partner or a DP—but refrain from being pulled into the dance by using the antidote described below.

There is a way out. Using simple yet effective spiritual practice, you can work wonders with your partner and your problems. This will also help you to navigate the environment of any DP. The antidote is simply to quiet the mind and align with stillness. This will dissolve the pain body, even while it's active in someone else and they are attacking you.

In the movie, *Eat, Pray, Love*, Julia Roberts's character travels to India in an attempt to learn how to meditate and quiet the mind. Over dinner one night, while overhearing friends speak about the movie, I became aware of their confusion as to what is actually required to quiet the mind. They seemed to feel that the path to a quiet mind was an extraordinarily difficult one. It is common to refute the simplicity of the process, but remember, as I've said, it's the *mind* that believes this is difficult. In reality, *you* already exist in this quiet state. All that is needed is to uncover your natural quietude that is already there but covered up by mental noise. That is precisely what this chapter is all about.

Most people's minds never stop thinking. Pay attention to the chronic nature of your own mind and you will see that this is the case. Once recognized, consciousness (you) begins to awaken from its dream state. But until this awakening begins in earnest, you are an unaware sleepwalker. Enlightenment occurs when you are ripe, spiritually, which is when there is a decline in compulsive thought until the silent gaps between thoughts are longer and longer. Effective spiritual practice uncovers consciousness that is pure presence, the still life force. When there are more frequent gaps between thoughts than there is noisy compulsive thinking, you become more fully aligned with that life force and become more of who you already *are*. This is the process of spiritual awakening.

As a way to add or uncover consciousness, Eckhart Tolle developed a simple but effective spiritual practice that I have expanded upon and used in my daily life in order to awaken spiritually. It is powerful yet simple and allows the student of spirituality to awaken consciously. Heretofore, it has been more common to awaken spontaneously as a result of intense mental or physical suffering or when on the brink of suicide. When used regularly as a spiritual practice, transformation in all areas of life occurs.

There are three gateways, or points of entry, that can be accessed to align with pure presence. When this alignment occurs, the mind cannot help but become quiet, at least to some degree. With practice, the mind can stop entirely from compulsive thought, but then thought is able to be picked up again and used as a tool when needed.

When your mind is quiet, a deep sense of peace and serenity is uncovered no matter the outward circumstances. This deep sense of peace and serenity is the essence of *you*. It is the same as your true self, the invisible life force that animates the physical body. It feels wonderful to uncover fully more of what you already *are*, but has been obscured. This is what happens when inner stillness is accessed, and the mind's noisy chatter is shut down.

*When aligned with inner stillness, the present moment is easily embraced because inner stillness or presence is the present moment.*

Rather than habitually resisting life, you will feel at peace with it, no matter what's happening in your environment. Then it can be said that you are flowing with the river's current, rather than pushing at the river from the bank.

When you align with *inner* stillness, or when you align with the *outer* stillness in your immediate environment, the mind becomes still. With either one, inner or outer, you align with the present moment and are at peace. Stillness increases the energy field that makes up the physical body, and this inner energy field expands and becomes more apparent. Effective spiritual practice gradually increases this energy field, which in turn helps to dissolve the pain body. Then, trapped energy that has been stored by the pain body is released for use by *you*.

When some of the energy which was previously trapped by the pain body has been reclaimed by you, the degree of enhancement to your inner sense of well-being, as well as to your physical body, is extraordinarily powerful and beneficial. Imagine if there was a way to instantaneously bathe yourself in a pool of deep sublime peace, while simultaneously connecting you so directly to your own power that you actually feel *yourself* to be a virtual power station. When this happens, you don't have to work at being in the present moment, because you already *are* the present moment. At that moment you and the source of life are one. You have reclaimed *you.* There is a deep recognition of yourself as perfect and alive, and you would readily agree that absolutely nothing at all matters, because all is right with the world to a degree that has never been previously experienced by you. In turn, your body begins to pulse with energy, as though the power floodgate to your cells has been suddenly thrown open.

This process began to occur for me regularly; it created its own momentum, and I soon recognized how recovering this trapped energy actually invokes a transformation on all levels. Although this didn't initially last very long, suddenly there was no question that, if I could find a way to reclaim that state of bliss, I could revamp every area of my life.

For example, once while driving along Pacific Coast Highway with Jeannette, the most extraordinary deep peace suddenly washed over me. This was of an altogether different order of sublime peace than I had ever experienced. As I looked out at the ocean, and particularly the wide-open space above the ocean, I *knew* it to be the same as *me.* My mind stopped thinking. Tears streamed down my cheeks. Rather than merely *thinking* about this as a *concept*, here was an actual *experience* of it; meaning that instantaneously the deep source of life that powered the sky and ocean was experienced as the very same one as the *I*, that *I am.*

By the time we arrived at Jeannette's home an hour later, my sense of peace was so deep that I noticed an immediate impact on all the electronic devices in the house. Since the electromagnetic field of my outer body was vibrating so much faster as a result of this peace, it cannot help but to cause some disruption to electrical appliances and electronic devices. My cell phone stopped working, as did a CD player, and several lights. Although these disruptions were temporary, I noted an extraordinary inner power that had heretofore remained unavailable to me until I began to reclaim it from my pain body.

In addition to this vital, pulsing energy that permeated my body and a deeply profound inner calm, I noticed an immediate change in my skin color and physical energy level. Problems that had been bothering me suddenly seemed meaningless, and I now had a clear ability to recognize right action with right timing and clear intent. Confusion dissipated. An indescribable feeling of love for all settled upon me. If you have ever experienced that overwhelming deep pleasure of being in love when all the world is right—and *everyone* in it—then imagine living like this all the time. Annoyances, irritations, and worries vanished as though I had stepped into a new world where they do not exist. That is, until Jeannette began to yell loudly at me, and as if I were Cinderella changing back into a pauper, my peaceful existence vanished and I glared at her as though she had just stolen my sanity.

It was then that I realized that there had to be a way to hold on to that state of bliss and equanimity, despite whomever or whatever seemingly impinged upon it. This kind of deep abiding peace, I sensed, could not be that transient. It was there permanently to be aligned with, and I had to consciously claim it or not. From that point on, I became determined to adopt the stance of the silent witness and align with presence during Jeannette's angry outbursts. She would still frequently yell at me, but I would now calmly observe her in a state of the alert witness by accessing stillness as described below. In this way, she ceased to have power to yank my sense of peace around like a puppy on a leash. My goal became to reclaim sufficient vital energy from my pain body, which would allow me to remain at my truest state of peace and well-being, no matter what.

If the present moment is the same as stillness, which is the same as the life force, when you align more fully with what you already are—inner or outer stillness and the present moment—then *more* of your natural energy is accessed and you feel better on all levels. Enlightenment is gradually uncovered as your present state of being. When any of the three gateways are accessed, you are pointed directly toward the heart of the awakening process. When you do this daily, it starts to feel quite natural until it becomes your permanent state.

The three gateways can be accessed separately, but it doesn't matter where you start because they all point you in the same direction. The three gateways are:

- the inner energy field of the body

- the breath

- the present moment

Each gateway is very easy to access and once entered, connects up with the other two.

## The Inner Energy Field of the Body

We have now identified the cause of most suffering as the noisy mind, with its inherent compulsive thought. If the mind is active, yet does not produce suffering for the bearer or those around him, then it is being constructively used in its proper context: as a tool and then put down, rather than the tool taking over the operator as it does for most people.

*Almost everyone knows of someone who is considered difficult to be around. The cause of the discomfort, the "difficult" aspect of the person, is the noisy mind's obsessive need to chatter about, fixate on, and attempt to solve minutia.*

The energy frequency of compulsive thought is very low and dense. Imagine an airplane propeller that, when rotating slowly, is very visible. You can see it; it is easily detectable. It is a loud uncomfortable form. Words, because they too are forms, are actual matter. Lots of words and mental thought equal a low energetic output. It's heavy and feels like sludge, especially when compared to the very high, fine vibration of stillness that vibrates so quickly that it's actually silent. Like the airplane propeller that increases in speed until it is invisible, a quiet mind increases and expands the body's energy field, which feels more comfortable to be around.

While the physical body is matter, there exists another of those strange paradoxes, that when comprehended, can be used with incredibly healing results:

*The inner energy field of the physical body is the highest, fastest vibrating energy available, because it is precisely the same energy as the source of you. In fact, it is you: It is the same as life. The inner energy field of the body is that warm, tingly feeling inside you.*

The quiet mind and the inner energy field of the body are synonymous with life in its purest expression. This is why stillness is so healing. You are simply adding more of yourself. This inner energy field of the body, when first detected, has a gentle sensation. You can sense it as a subtle warmth, or tingling energy. It is pure life force. When you consciously focus on this energetic vibration, the speed of the vibration is increased and expanded.

The same principle applies to the silent essence that makes up you. When you place your attention on it, it increases and expands, simply by having been focused upon. This vibration produces an actual sense of serenity because the "you" that is pure essence has now become conscious of its real self. This self-realization is powerfully transformative because you have finally recognized the essence of who you really are. Imagine if a lion believed it was a goat. When the lion finally looks into a lake and sees his reflection as that of a lion, he can never again live from the perspective of a goat. The myth has been shattered and a new, higher level of existence reveals itself.

You can finally recognize and utilize your inherent "lion" characteristics, which were already there but entirely obscured by a false understanding of your true nature. When you become aware of your true characteristics, anxiety and suffering dissolve because you no longer subscribe to "rules and regulations" produced and upheld by a goat society. The lion can still maneuver and function in the world of goats, but is not *part* of that world. "Be *in* the world but not *of* it."

Try this exercise now to become aware of the inner energy field of your own body: Start by closing your eyes. Although this is not necessary, at first it will help you to clearly identify this still presence within you as you become familiar with the practice. Become still and focus on your right hand. Feel the warmth of it. Perhaps you can sense a very faint tingling sensation. Can you feel the life inside it? Once felt, even if the sensation is very slight, switch your focus to the left hand and its inner energy field. When you can sense both hands, now add your right foot and focus on it. Then add the left foot. Once you can feel all four appendages without moving at all, then "fill in" the rest of your body, so that you are now focusing on the inner energy field of the entire body. Feel how it vibrates and pulses with life. This pulsing, tingly feeling is pure source. When you focus on it, you have accessed life itself and you have now aligned yourself with it.

At any time of the day or night, you can use this exercise while you are doing some other activity. For example, while walking across the room, you can focus on the hands and feet, and then "add" the entire body, focusing on its inner energy field. If a thought interrupts you, become the "watcher" of your mind. Simply observe the thought, and then return to the exercise. Because *you* are not the same as your thoughts, you now have a conscious technique in which you can practice being the observer of your thoughts. This is the process of dis-identifying with the mind's activity.

Often, just as you are becoming comfortable with this process, the mind may squeal in protest that this is a stupid, simplistic exercise that is diverting its time from solving more important issues. That's okay. Just observe how the mind shuns simplicity and adores complexity, and carry on with the exercise. No matter what the mind decides to think, you now know that you don't have to agree with those thoughts, that you are not your thoughts. Just observe how the mind keeps thinking. This is tremendously helpful in producing transformative healing for chronic negative mental activity.

For example, while grocery shopping with Jeannette, I push her wheelchair down the aisles of the market and focus on the inner energy field of my body. Then Jeannette begins to whine because, like a three-year-old, she wants to buy one thing after another and attempts to heave multiple items into the basket on her lap. Rather than reacting, I allow her to both moan and add to the basket, while continuing this inner focus. Once we get to the check-stand, I simply hand the unwanted items to the clerk and say "no thank you," despite Jeannette's ever-increasing protests. Jeannette then tries to stand up to engage with me more fully, but I continue to keep my focus on the inner energy field of my body. Thus, I am aligned with presence and I am alert and aware but not at all reactive. Perhaps I allow the purchase of a banana or a bottle of lotion and hand them to her, but the pulse of life belongs to peace, not drama, in this environment. There is no tactic by the pain body that can divert one from dedicated spiritual practice, providing that you are well aware of how the pain body dance tries by its insistence to divert your attention to its addictive voice. Now let's continue with your practice.

Return your focus to the inner energy field of the body. Again feel the warmth of it as it expands in your awareness. In some people, one part of the body may tingle more strongly than another area but this does not matter. Simply hold your attention on this energy field and you will notice that the mind immediately quiets. If a thought disrupts your attention, simply notice it without judgment and return your focus again to the inner energy field. If a second thought emerges, notice how the mind attempts to lure you away from this practice, and instead, again place your attention on the inner energy field. You will notice that the mind immediately starts searching for some problem that it says is more important. It wants you to focus on trouble. The mind prefers to be active and noisy.

Because this higher energy vibration is not being obscured by noisy thought, it is a very powerful healing balm. As you focus on it, others can feel *your* energetic vibration and it's experienced as pleasurable to be around, although few are able to identify why. Like the airplane propeller, it vibrates so fast that the denseness of the outer physical body also benefits and its own vibration will also increase. When focus on this inner energy field is sustained, even for just a few seconds, you will become calm, at peace, and grounded in a sense of alert awareness. When this practice becomes more comfortable, you can lengthen these gaps between mental thought so that you spend more and more time out of each day aligned with stillness—your essence.

In contrast, the busy mind is anxious, worried, concerned, and compulsive. Of course, the sufferer's compulsive mind doesn't *recognize* its own compulsivity and minutia-focused obsession, but instead feels superior in its ability to identify and solve problems and thus feels smart.

When you consciously switch focus from the inner energy field to the mind, an altogether different order of thought becomes possible. Thought, or the quality of your thinking, becomes calmer, but also more efficient and appropriately perfect to identify and solve problems with more finesse. Try it and you will see that this is the case. Focus on the inner energy field of the body, but then on something that is "important" like a pending dispute with your landlord. After a few minutes, return focus again to the inner energy field alone, and then back to the problem, and so on. Suddenly, thought is now infused with source, so it becomes more effective and creative, because thought is now immersed in equanimity.

But take note, when you first try this back-and-forth practice by alternating between your focus on the body's inner energy field and then on thinking, as soon as you "allow" thought to have its way, you may discover that you soon forget to quiet it again. This is the goal of the mind, to permanently restore your attention back on compulsive thinking.

In addition, you can practice *simultaneously* focusing on the inner energy field and also directing the mind to a particular task. Try this experiment now: Focus on what your plans are for this evening. Take a moment to consider what you will wear or what must still be done to be ready for this evening. Perhaps you still have to purchase groceries for dinner or dessert as a dinner gift. Now, at the same time, focus on the inner energy field of the body. Notice how you are able to successfully focus on both. This exercise may seem like a waste of time, and you can be certain that your mind will insist that it is; however, you have now added the healing power of stillness to the thought process. Not only will you feel calm and present while planning a future event, but the energy field that makes up the physical body is being expanded and reclaimed from the pain body.

Once you have practiced doing this, now identify some problem that you have not been able to solve. Once you have this thought or dilemma firmly in mind, simultaneously focus on the inner energy field of the body. This process allows the "problem" to be surrounded by "space" in order to infuse it with the life force. You may be surprised to discover that soon after, a solution suddenly emerges. But even if no solution is immediately apparent, you are becalmed and neither this problem nor any other can move you from your peace. In truth, any right solution is borne from your essence, not from thinking, although thought can now take up the solution and effectively take the next step with it.

This process is ideal when used for effective listening, particularly when you are listening to a person whose pain body is active, such as any DP's. This exercise produces near magical applications for staying present when there is chaos in your midst. This single practice can prevent your own pain body from being triggered into an active state, and also, it allows you to more appropriately respond to anyone, whether the other person is engrossed in a negative emotional state or not. You will be able to solve problems more effectively and efficiently, and will not cause stress for yourself or others. In this way, use of the mind is not compulsive with an unconscious need to stay active and bothered.

Our specific task is how to focus on the inner energy field of the body, which in turn dissolves suffering and transforms a person into a higher order of being. As a result, an increased level of aliveness becomes palpable. Not only will your emotions cease their relentless journey between extreme highs and lows, but the energy field of your physical body expands substantially. This is experienced as increased physical well-being, higher and more accessible intelligence, the reduction of pain and illness, and a greater ability to enjoy a simple life without need for constant distractions and amusement.

Although seeking physical release through sex, or attempting to "add" something such as food, drugs, or alcohol, is actually an unconscious need to fill up on presence, these means cannot achieve this end and can never satisfy us over the long-term. Once mental noise and its attendant emotional swings decrease, you can enjoy physical sensations without becoming lost in them. Prior to awakening, physical sensation is sought as an unconscious need for peace. Once that has been established within, sensation can still be enjoyed but it is not a requirement for wholeness. When you combine higher energies with physical sensation simultaneously, a calming and lovely mutual experience of peace can be experienced, but you will not get lost in it and it is not needed in order to feel satisfied.

## The Breath

Sometimes, prior to awakening, when the environment feels stressful or you are tired and it is more difficult to slow mental thought sufficiently to focus on anything else, you can use the second gateway.

Since a solution of sufficient power is needed to dissolve mental noise and its attendant pain body, this second gateway, the breath, offers a precise and perfect antidote. It immediately connects you with the first and third gateways. Its superior ability to immediately quiet the mind and align you with "right action" and "right response" can be used consciously, again and again until it becomes a habit.

Simply take a deep breath and focus on it as it fills your lungs. Allow the breath to take your focus inside. Notice the slight pause following full exhale, prior to the lungs filling again with air.

Focus on this slight pause, noticing the stillness of the body and the quieting mind. After the first deep breath, take several more conscious breaths, inhaling deeply. Because the breath is invisible, it is a "no-thing." This means that the breath—in the same way that space is a no-thing—is the *opposite* of matter or form, and is thus closer to alignment with your life force. Like the inner energy field of the body, the breath is another aspect of you that can assist in better alignment with presence.

Continue to focus on the breath—taking big, deep, slow breaths—and follow it to the inside of you, to the inner energy field of the body. By focusing on the breath and the inner energy field simultaneously, thought immediately becomes still. Right action can now be put into effect because the proper order of response has been followed. First focus on the breath or the inner energy field of the body, and *then* respond as necessary. Or, you may find that the highest response is no response at all but simply to remain in a state of alert awareness. Your powerful inner essence has been uncovered by quieting the mind. Now the "river of life" becomes more apparent, and appropriate response is more easily recognized and dispensed with finesse, if it is necessary at all.

In addition, when presence is accessed via these gateways, your deep abiding stillness is wonderfully contagious when practiced in the presence of others. Stillness is synonymous with the essence of life; indeed, stillness is life itself. The more steeped in the accessible essence of life, the more helpful your presence is to others. They will benefit by your proximity to them, but will have no idea why or how they enjoy your company. Your own palpable essence is felt by others and they are immediately reminded of their own, same essence.

In my role as caregiver, this was the practice I used hundreds of times daily when Jeannette's Alzheimer's was in its most aggressive and confrontational stage. For two solid years prior to awakening, I relied on this practice as though it were my only life preserver in a tumultuous, stormy ocean. It didn't matter whether we were in the car, shopping mall, or in the kitchen. Whether or not her pain body became active, or if we were simply together outside in the garden, I was vigilant in holding fast to this practice and did not allow anything to dissuade me from its use. Not only is it effective in preventing your pain body from being triggered (until it is dissolved), but its use also increases the energy field of the physical body, and so there are two powerful processes occurring simultaneously. You are aligning with the life force, but also the energy field of the physical body is increasing and expanding. It is the most effective and appropriate response to anyone who is attacking you, whether verbally or physically, because it immediately puts you in touch with the needed "right action" or "right" words to handle the situation.

Once while pulling into a gas station near a busy airport, in the days when Jeannette still had her physical agility, she jumped out of the car and began to dart around the other cars that were pulling in and out of the station. After attempting to direct and contain her to no avail, I recognized that this was a crisis because the other drivers did not know that she was easily confused and could suddenly walk in front of their car. Placing my attention on my breath, I allowed it to take my attention inside to the inner energy field of my body. Immediately, inner stillness was acting through me and directed me to quickly act. By running over to each individual driver, I directed a "cease driving" interval of sufficient duration to recapture Jeannette and put her into the vehicle. I then activated the auto lock feature of my car. Even though my body appeared to be in fast action, my mind was still and it is this stillness which manages the scene, not our busy mental chatter.

Such right action is sponsored by your essence as it aligns with the life force, rather than the ego with its inherent self-seeking agenda or negative emotional reactions of fear or anger. When right action is identified and put into place, everyone benefits to the highest degree, rather than just one person. Otherwise, the busy mind with its ever-present egoic needs attempts to analyze needs from its own perspective, and so its conclusions can almost always be counted on to be self-serving and thus limited. Using this practice does not mean that taking fast, decisive, and effective action becomes wrong or unnecessary. In fact, if such action is required, it will be that much more aligned with the "flow of the river," and it will thus be more effective; however, such fast action must *follow* the alignment with essence, not be introduced prior to aligning with it. Once aligned with essence, further action can then be taken with a better result for all concerned.

For example, when in the presence of a DP, the moment that you discern a verbal attack or reaction is forthcoming, immediately reserve some of your attention for the inner energy field of the body. Immediately, take a deep breath and direct some of your focus to your breathing. *Do not give all of your focus to "problems" or to the DP.* Always hold back some of your attention to focus on your breath and the inner energy field of the body, simultaneously. This practice is the key to awakening in the midst of everyday circumstances and problematic environments.

During moments of stress is precisely when you can most benefit by accessing any of the three gateways, particularly the first and second, because they will automatically align you with the peace of the present moment. Remember, even when chaos appears to be present, stillness can always be aligned with from the core of your being, no matter the degree of turmoil in the environment.

As you become more practiced in accessing these first two gateways, your thoughts slow down considerably at all times because space consciousness has been added and stillness takes up residence in you.

Using the three gateways, you are still able to think, but you can buffer your thinking by first placing your attention on the breath and inner energy field. This way, your stillness permeates your thinking as all of you is rooted in consciousness. Creativity is at its highest using this practice because brilliant creativity is not borne from mind activity. It is borne from pure source, which then uses the mind as a vehicle to put that perfect creative impulse into worldly expression.

## The Present Moment

The third gateway is surrendering to the "perfection" of the present moment, no matter the circumstances that arise. When aligning with the inner source via the first two gateways, you are actually aligning with the present moment itself, although this may not seem to be the case. Because thought is actually form, the spacious "nothingness" of the inner energy field of the body and also the breath are its opposite and counteract it. You become calm. The mind has been stilled, at least to some degree. When this occurs, you have become aligned with the present moment itself. *A becalmed ability to surrender to what is has happened.* Because compulsive thought concerns itself with the past and future, the present moment is usually avoided, and thus suffering occurs.

The third gateway involves moving *directly* to acceptance of the present moment, just as it is. This means that you behold whatever situation is presenting itself, and don't attempt to resist it or react negatively to it.

*This happens whether you are beholding freeway gridlock; the angry, resistant behavior of another person; bad or upsetting news;*

*your burned dinner; or physical discomfort or pain. Prior to respond-ing or attempting action of any kind, first allow what is to be as it already is in all of its perfection.*

As you notice the keys inside your locked car or the roadblock up ahead, take a deep breath and *relax.* It is what it is. Since the mind is incapable of accepting the present moment, it will "goat" you into getting frustrated or angry, which effectively elevates it to a position of moral superiority over the circumstances. This is the world in which the lion erroneously believes it is a goat, in the same way that you believe that you are your mind. Your awakening occurs when you recognize that you are the source of the mind, not the mind itself. The goat has awakened from its nightmare where circumstances are fought against moment to moment and hour to hour. Only the lion recognizes that the present moment can never be fought against without producing suffering.

## Making Friends with the Present Moment

In my job as caregiver to Jeannette, as she entered the last phase of the disease, the nature of my duties expanded as her state declined. Her husband of forty-five years was holding up quite well under the stress due to his own intuitive surrendering to that which could not be controlled; however, it was evident that he would benefit from whatever help I could provide seven days a week. As a busy professional, he worked the usual workweek, returning home in the evening to care for his wife. Occasionally, he had work requiring out-of-town travel. During that time, I would stay at their home with Jeannette. When her condition worsened, I eventually moved into their house.

Despite having had virtually no exposure to spiritual prac-tice, Jeannette's husband frequently responded to others' chronic worrying about the scope of his potential stress by reminding them that "it is what it is." He even has a baseball cap emblazoned with these words. Consequently, his calm demeanor often surprised me, particularly during his wife's relentless, highly charged attempts to pull him into drama. Although few people could avoid feeling some frustration or exasperation while caring for an Alzheimer's patient, her husband became practiced at experiencing remarkable calm in the face of constant challenges. Whether or not he was aware of it, he increasingly demonstrated the presence of a practiced student of spirituality, and became a model of accepting the present moment as it is without negative reaction. Also, be became quite practiced at noticing how another's pain body would attempt to pull him into drama.

During this period, when it was evident that Jeannette would need even more care than she was already receiving, he discussed with me possible solutions to the expanding workload. As was my usual response, I replied that I felt rested, with a pervasive sense of well-being no matter the outward circumstances, and could handle weekends as well. In truth, I make no distinction between days that I am "working" or days that I am "off"—in the way that I feel or the degree of my sense of well-being. My awakening had produced a distinct inability to distinguish a difference between "working" and "playing." This is not an issue of semantics; I truly cannot identify any source of stress, even if I look for it. When one becomes the silent witness to life circumstances by adopting a stance of alert awareness, no stress can be produced. As a result, logging hours on the weekend didn't feel like "work." So when I offered to work the next Sunday by preparing a meal for them or to take care of Jeannette on what would normally be my day off, I expressed that it would not bother me in the least. Despite having already worked a seventy-hour workweek, it had no bearing whatsoever as to the level of restfulness or calm that I experienced at week's end.

Because my intention was to help transition Jeannette and her husband through the entire process of her illness, no matter how many years that took, I already suspected that more help would be needed as her condition worsened. Although Jeannette had now entered the final phase of Alzheimer's, there was no way of knowing how much longer my help would be needed. My employment was now entering its third year.

Normally her husband was somewhat doubtful about my claims of well-being after completing a challenging workweek. But this time, as I again offered to help out on Sunday, he replied that he understood, by virtue of having watched a documentary the previous night that explored the mental state of female prostitutes. These women had also reported that it didn't really matter what their bodies were doing, that they had found a way to make "work" tolerable. They conceived of it unemotionally, as a means to an end, and they were okay with it while it was happening. One prostitute in particular had admitted that she had dissociated herself from the unpleasant task by focusing instead on what was *next* or what she would *gain* in the future as a result of her present circumstances.

As we chuckled at the comparison between my job description and theirs, I denied that the process of "handling" the present moment was similar. To the contrary, although there appeared to be no resistance on the prostitutes' part, in actual fact, they were far from reveling in a chronic state of peace and inner well-being. In actuality, the one prostitute was in abject *resistance* to the present moment, although outwardly she appeared to be calm and nonreactive. Her awareness and focus were *outside and away* from her "work"—the act of sex. She was virtually "not there," although her body was.

Effective spiritual practice is entirely different, and one that is ultimately the only true guarantee of lasting inner peace. I experience a deep satisfaction in the present moment, not wishing that it will soon pass and be replaced by something else. So practiced had I now become in aligning with the present moment without resistance that I often did not need to be consciously focused on the first two gateways to help align me with the present moment. It was happening automatically. Instead, I would focus solely on the satisfaction in what I was "doing." In this way, I was making friends with the present moment.

For example, as I walk across the kitchen from the table to the refrigerator, I focus on the act of walking. I am aware of my breath and the feel of the floor beneath my feet. The walking itself is thoroughly enjoyable and it alone holds the promise for peace. There is no future event that is in mind that will be better than my walking from the table to the refrigerator.

In the case of my having already logged a sixty- or seventy-hour workweek, there is no residual at all from having done so. As a result, when I arrived at their house on a Sunday following this schedule to offer to prepare dinner and wash the dishes, it did not at all feel as though I were logging "overtime." In fact, not only would it *not* feel burdensome, I would actually enjoy it.

For example, try this yourself. While preparing a salad for your meal by cutting up vegetables, feel the perfect peace and sense the joy at the beauty and simplicity that comes with just chopping the carrots. *It* is the actual goal, not any future benefit like eating it. Cutting the vegetables is the goal itself. Rather than trying to get away from the body when doing mundane things like doing the laundry or vacuuming, lasting inner peace results from fully inhabiting the inner energy field of the body no matter what it is doing. When you do simple tasks, use the breath by breathing in deeply to take you to the inner energy field of the body. Take many, long deep breaths until you are grounded in your essence.

This means that whether you are walking across the kitchen, taking a bath, driving a car, paying for groceries at the checkout counter, or having a conversation, your attention is placed on the action that is being performed *only*, without allowing thoughts to be diverted elsewhere. You can still remain aware of your surroundings, or in my case, I can still take care of Jeannette. But your focus includes your breath and the inner energy field of the body; however, you don't *think* about it; simply be aware of it.

This practice allows you to stay fully rooted in presence at all times. This way, dis-identification with thought activity becomes a normal way of living and you will no longer be a reaction machine, emotionally responding to the madness of the world, or dissociating from it as the "working girls" do.

In the example of my preparing dinner and then cleaning up the kitchen, there is no future being pondered while chopping or scrubbing. There is no payoff of a better outcome that is promised as a result of the chopping or cleaning. The chopping and cleaning itself are the goals. The knife and the carrots and my hands and the salad are my entire world at that moment. There is no other world, so to speak, that is better than this one involving chopping up vegetables. There is still focus on the breath—deep, slow breaths in and out—but there is nothing else that I would rather be doing. This is what is meant when the practice of Zen challenges the seeker to undertake "one thing at a time." If some focus is reserved for the breath and the inner energy field of the body, because it is space, a "no-thing," then you have diverted chronic thinking away from an alignment with form or matter.

This is why everything that is attempted or undertaken becomes so effortless when you are fully immersed in the present moment. It is why normally unpleasant tasks become so pleasurable. It is also why you can better connect to other people or express yourself creatively—you are aligned with the source of all life in the present moment.

*With no inner resistance to subdue natural enthusiasm, boredom or monotony is virtually impossible to experience.*

Existing fully in the present moment means to simply place your attention fully on whatever is being attended to at the moment. You effectively become a silent witness to whatever happens or arises. By remaining in a state of alert awareness, you are the watcher of life, no longer a reactor to it. This produces a profound deep spiritual pleasure, which is lasting and replaces the shallow pleasure sought by the pain body seeking to gain satisfaction from its addiction to drama. Since most of us have not been aware that the mind is compulsively focused on past or possible future events, it may take some practice to simply do one thing at a time; however, I do not mean to suggest that more "future" is needed to feel becalmed. Right this moment, reading these words, let it become your world and you are one with the present.

This practice can be done anywhere. If you are driving your car, simply place your attention on the road. As thoughts pop into your head, you can either take a deep breath and focus on breathing, or focus on the inner energy field of the body and your thoughts will immediately subside. Notice how, when the mind is slowed or stopped, the eyes are able to observe things on the road, but the mental commentary is absent. The eyes become like the innocent eyes of a baby. There is no mental judgment or comparing and contrasting. The eyes simply take in whatever is there without criticism, judgment, or resistance. The eyes see the traffic jam, and simply observe it with no negative labeling. When you do this, possibly for the first time in a very long time, you are now absent of compulsive thought. This is the same innocent state of being in which a baby resides, or a Zen Master.

We have all observed the indescribably beautiful essence that is noticeable when you look into the eyes of a baby. The infant looks back at you with no mental commentary because its mind is not yet active and there is no thinking. When your eyes meet, it is as if there is an exchange of purity that is transformative. You have become aware of the degree to which the child is so beautifully aligned with stillness, the perfect pure essence that is life. This is the exact same state that your practice will have you consciously aligned with and that is the same presence as the lovely innocent baby.

This is the process to peace. You will become so aligned with what you are doing, that the present moment actually turns into a meditation and it is thus transformed. When you find the present moment to be acceptable, you make friends with life. In turn, life becomes friendly with you, and surprising and miraculous opportunities present themselves almost magically. Once chronic and compulsive resistance is dissolved, an ever-present state of well-being is uncovered.

As the three gateways to peace are accessed and as this spiritual practice is implemented daily, you may notice how the mind wants to interrupt you and attempts to throw up an urgent problem that it says needs your attention right now. The mind will be very cunning and will do a mental scan of all your vulnerable emotional weaknesses until it locates the perfect "thing" that will stop your practice so that you can focus on "it."

But knowing how the mind attempts to continue its compulsive habit, you do not allow it to divert you. Once momentum is gained, you become more practiced in denying its attempt to commandeer you. As you notice the noisy, cunning mind trying to divert you, keep coming back and focus on any of the three gateways. You will find that the mind eventually will surrender to the inevitable and accept its "important" role as a tool.

This spiritual practice is so enormously healing, so immediately energizing, that if you were to continue this practice for one year—accepting that there will be natural stops and restarts—you could completely transform your life.

## The Peace That Makes Up the Present Moment

On the weekends while at my own home, prior to Jeannette's condition worsening, I earnestly applied the above spiritual practice under the shade of an enormous palm tree on my mother's property in Malibu. During that time, I was not only practicing accessing the three gateways, but also I began to identify and unravel all the areas of "need" that my ego said that I could not live without. The precise details of this exercise are described in chapter 7; however, prior to undertaking that additional exercise, it might first be helpful to recognize the "loud" peace and quiet that permeates every moment of the now. By focusing your attention on the stillness inherent in trees, flowers, and plants, you become aware of the same stillness within yourself. This was my practice on the weekends, during which I would simply "look" without comment at the palm tree overhead and the plants and flowers that were around me. There is bliss in observing and listening to the wind as it dances through the leaves of a tree, or how it ripples across a field of grass. Even if some man-made noise should arise in the environment, you can still become aware of the stillness that remains, that has and will always be there. No matter how loud or busy your environment, there is a stunning stillness that undergirds it.

This is the case even when there are many people present, like at a football stadium or shopping mall. One adopts the stance of becoming the silent witness, especially in noisy or chaotic environments. The stillness is readily accessed by using the first or second gateways, the inner energy field of the body and the breath, which are always aligned with this undergirding presence. Once identified, this peaceful stillness can be detected and aligned with no matter your location or experience. To this day, one of my fondest experiences is to simply observe and to listen to the wind in the trees. Surely, the ability to align with stillness is the practice that the saints and sages through history used during extreme moments of despair or suffering. Without becoming familiar with its application, the *conscious* practice or way to enlightenment may not be possible.

Although many hikers, nature lovers, or outdoor athletes will readily recognize the power of being aware of and immersed in the stillness within natural settings, there is a nuance to its effective use that is of a different order than what most nature lovers experience.

In essence, you begin this practice outdoors; or indoors if there are any plants, flowers, or trees nearby. You simply look deeply at a flower, plant, or a tree without labeling its attributes, and notice the intense surrender to stillness that permeates it, even in a breeze. Become aware of the lovely beauty in its simplicity.

Notice how it is alive, but that its survival does not entail any struggle; it does not "work" at its aliveness. It simply *is*. Notice how the flower exists completely in stillness. If there is any sound in the environment, the flower is nonetheless still, connected to its source and is quiet and alive. One of the most stunningly beautiful demonstrations of presence is to observe with a quiet mind the rustling of the wind through the leaves of a tree or through a field of flowers. By making this quiet observation, the power of your presence comes alive because you are now observing the characteristic of *you* (your true essence) *in* the flower. Consciousness is becoming aware of itself, and it feels joyous.

Unless and until you are able to comfortably sit in stillness and notice the quiet in an environment, you are not yet experiencing the rise of consciousness. To be able to become aware of the myriad ways that nature displays stillness is an extraordinary spiritual practice. Normally we take it for granted that a tree is still, given its girth and rootedness. Yet, when you look beyond the assumptions of what a tree is, it is indeed quite extraordinary that a living thing such as a tree is so rooted in being, that even if you were to chop it down, its formless gentle stillness would remain undisturbed. This is one of the deepest spiritual practices you can apply. Yes, you survive death and so does the tree.

The power of this practice first became apparent to me when, after looking silently without mental commentary upon a beautiful tree in my garden every day for many months, after closely observing its lovely red berry clusters, I began to care for the tree by watering it and clipping its branches. I admired the way that it sought sunlight by growing its branches out over neighboring shrubs.

Then, one hot day I came out to water it, and I was shocked to my core to see that someone had actually taken an axe and chopped the entire tree down. There wasn't a trace of the former tree, except for the stump. Startled, I spun around, looking for signs of fallen branches, or sawdust, or clippings. Who did this? How could this have happened in the garden that I so frequented, without my knowing about it?

It turned out that my mother had instructed my brother to cut it down because it was considered problematic and also thought to be dying. This was a turning point in my spiritual practice as I beheld the stump of the tree, and how it didn't seem to have suffered any emotional reaction whatsoever to its death. The stump, quiet in the sunlight, seemed mystically laughing at me, as if to say, "All forms are temporary, but the life that *underlies* them lives on forever."

At that moment I recognized that it is this inner life that, once aligned with, grows and expands in your experience, until your identification is to *it*, rather than the form. This realization startled me. How was it possible that a living thing could so easily surrender its life when events conspired to end it "too soon"? How could the tree stump seem so at peace sitting there in the sun, with the absence of its trunk, branches, and leaves, when I was so grieving its loss? My mind could find no answer, and so it stopped completely. Historically, sages have reported that during periods when their minds have stopped, extraordinary realizations occur and a complete dis-identification with mental activity happens.

This realization brought a deep recognition of the benefits of being aware of the stillness embodied in plants and flowers—or any stillness in nature—and how when you contemplate *outer* stillness, you then become aware of your *inner* stillness. Frequent alignment with stillness, whether inside or outside, uncovers presence more fully, and mental noise is no longer able to obscure the power of your true nature.

In addition, another wonderful opportunity to align with space occurs every time you are outside and can observe the big sky; however, instead of noticing all the "things" within the space, become aware of just the huge space itself. When you look up into a night sky, rather than looking at the stars, focus on the space in between them. When driving through a desert, become aware of the great expanse of space, and begin to notice that the space is the same as *you.*

## High Quality Bodily Movement and the Present Moment

When you move your body in any way, such as while walking across the kitchen floor, preparing a meal, steering an automobile, exercising, or brushing your teeth, place your attention on the inner energy field of the body and that of the breath. In so doing, you will be rooted in being, deeply connected to the life source, and as such will be permeated by a calm state and a deep sense of well-being. Although it is easy to associate stillness of the body with inner stillness, it is possible to remain completely still inwardly while the body is in fast motion. The key is, while the body is moving, no matter how quickly, to simultaneously place attention on the inner energy field of the body and also the breath. Indeed, although yoga practices and meditation often involve focusing one-pointed attention on some "thing," it is always more effective to focus attention on no-thing than on something. This means that the inner energy field of the body, which is space (no-thing), and the breath most closely relate to a no-thing, or space. Thus, one can have a busy body, but be at complete inner quiet because thought has been stilled. Conversely, one can be practicing meditation or yoga and the mind during that time can be quite noisy. The key is to become aware of the degree to which your own mind is active, whether the body is still or in fast movement.

You can also apply this practice to any sport such as tennis, surfing, golf, or rock climbing. Simply hold back some of your attention and focus on the breath and the inner energy field of the body, rather than focusing exclusively on the ball, the tool of your sport, or the mechanics of what your hands and arms are doing. Because you have probably already been well schooled in the mechanics of your sport, when you align with presence, *all* action increases in effectiveness because it now becomes life connecting to life. As you take up your sport, breathe in several long deep breaths and allow it to take you to the inner energy field of the body. Continue with your tennis game, or surfing, etc., but now, keep at least some of your focus on your breath and the inner energy field of the body and notice that your mind is quieting.

This practice can become very regular quite quickly and develops into a way of living that virtually guarantees a gentle and effective response to changing life circumstances and so-called problems. Fast action can still be taken when responding to emergencies, events, or challenging people; changes may still be initiated, but because you are so deeply grounded with the essence of life, you are not sucked into emotional reactivity by circumstances that most people find troubling. You are the silent witness and do not judge what occurs, nor do your reactions to life cause you trouble. This degree of permanent alignment with the present moment personifies the awakened state. It is a way of being that doesn't change with life's circumstances, which by their very nature are *always* changing. The magical application that most benefits you during moments of stress, is to immediately focus on taking long, deep breaths, and allow your breath to take you to the inner energy field of the body.

There is no physical activity that is too simple or too mundane that does not benefit from this alignment with presence. This is the point of spiritual practice: make it a way of life. Notice how still your mind, and thus your emotions, become when this practice is adopted in all areas of your life.

Most people's daily lives are spent in a chronic roller coaster of emotional reactions to one thing after another. No wonder most people feel chronically unwell and exhausted. If you come home after work and feel drained or worn out, then you are aligned with outer circumstances, not inner stillness. Since the mind exists to be offended by this or that disturbance and to unconsciously chase and react to problems, persistent peace and well-being are impossible following its lead. From the perspective of an awakened state, almost everyone is compulsively focusing on minutia and meaninglessness, but they seem to have no idea whatsoever what this is costing them.

Imagine your own reaction in visiting a psychiatric ward of a mental hospital and observing the extreme mental patterns of the sickest patients. You might shake your head in disbelief at the "acting out" of extreme mental illness. "What unnecessary suffering!" you might say to yourself, as the patients' negative emotional responses are observed as simply chronic mental chaos that cannot produce anything other than chronic suffering. From the perspective of an enlightened state, the pre-awakened "normal" state of being is equally misguided. The degree of anxiety, worry, and agitation that result from an unquestioned, chronically noisy mind can be as dysfunctional as that of any patient in a psychiatric hospital. It's not the degree of misalignment: you are either in the moment or not, and knocking your head against the wall is no different from polite faultfinding of minutia.

Once awakened, no thought goes unquestioned. Thoughts are recognized, when they cause suffering, to be lies; or at the very least, to be suspect until they are unraveled as a misunderstanding by a mind that can do nothing other than be offended. Thoughts are concepts and they produce an active mind. Even thoughts that contain seemingly altruistic ideas are still noisy thoughts. Simply attend a town meeting about how to obtain peace on Earth and you understand this point. Conversely, a deep sense of peace that arises from within is usually elicited by a feeling, not a thought, that comes from the source of life rather than from the ego. Again, a murderous thought is no different from a conceptual thought of universal brotherhood: busy mind or quiet mind is the choice.

## Are You in the Present Moment?

During the two years prior to my awakening while I was caring for Jeannette, it occurred to me that I really didn't know just how compulsive the normal state of my own mind really was. As I would watch her reacting to life circumstances, I kept noticing that I also continued to react to her reaction. There was an intellectual understanding that most people's minds were chronically focused on what had already happened—the past—or, their minds were focused on what was hoped for, or feared would take place in the future. Because other spiritual teachers such as Eckhart Tolle and Byron Katie had awakened suddenly and spontaneously as a result of intense emotional suffering without a conscious spiritual practice, it occurred to me that to do so consciously would require an accurate assessment of the obstacle to peace. If a noisy mind was that obstacle, just how noisy was it? Considering this, I began to wonder what the actual state of *my* mind was. It was time for me to find out.

I purchased a stopwatch at an athletics store, the kind that marathoners use to train for triathlons, and I set the alarm to sound every nine minutes, except while I slept. The first beep occurred, at which time I stopped to notice what was happening with my thoughts. Was I thinking of something that had already happened in the past? Or, was I contemplating some future event, or hoping for some positive outcome? Was I worried about something that hadn't even happened yet? After investigating the nature of my own thoughts in this manner for several days, I was shocked to discover just how non-stop my thinking actually was. Clearly, I could not deny that I could benefit from a quieter mind. Not only were my thoughts chronically active, but they were mostly repetitive. In addition, many thoughts had to do with the future or the past, even when I was physically involved in some activity. It seemed that my mind wasn't satisfied to engage in one activity at a time. It wanted to multi-task, to accomplish several things at once, all in the name of being more productive. Like everyone else's, my mind never stopped thinking.

As the alarm on my watch continued to sound every nine minutes, I became deeply aware of the nature of my thinking. No wonder I hadn't yet experienced self-realization. Having no idea just how bad the state of my mind really was, this recognition inspired an adherence to this practice of observing the status of my thoughts every nine minutes, for almost one entire year. In addition, every time the alarm would sound, I would focus on my breath and the inner energy field of the body. This would immediately align me with the perfection of the present moment. While in a noisy environment, I hung the watch from a chain around my neck to hear the alarm better. Even Jeannette's angry reaction to the sound of my watch, hands on hips, demanding "What's that sound?" produced yet another opportunity for me to stay aligned with presence, even as she reacted to my spiritual practice.

Eventually, it became an ingrained habit to be aware of what was going on in my mind, and then to quiet it by initially taking in many long deep breaths, and then allowing my breath to "take" me to the inner energy field of my body. In this way, I fully recognized the degree to which my thoughts manipulated my state of being. After using this practice with a stopwatch for a while, there came a time when the alarm would sound, but I was *already* focused on my breath and inner energy field of the body. This way, I was already fully aligned with the present moment and it was becoming a vital, life-enhancing habit.

As was stated previously, arguing against what has already happened is dysfunction of the highest order. The alarm on my watch initiated an awareness of just how often I was arguing mentally about what had already happened. I was quite shocked to discover just how often I caught myself trying to "get out" of the present moment by hoping to get into the next one. A frustrated response to what *is* cannot *change* what already is. Once the inherent "is-ness" of the present moment is accepted without denial or resistance, then change can be initiated, remedies can be installed, or strategies can be implemented. By using the watch's alarm as a tool, I became aware of the great need to improve, and was motivated to shift the entire way that I operated in the world.

*The reason why nonresistance of the present moment is so powerfully transformative is because acceptance of the now is contrary to the goals of the mind with its focus on past and future. Dissolving negative patterns of thought activity involves dismantling its preferences for denial of the now.*

When the mind is focused on the future, it wants to get out of the present moment and get to a "future moment" as fast as possible. The mind is angry with the present moment and wants a *different* moment altogether. This is dysfunctional in the extreme, but the normal way that most people respond to life. The DP frequently demands that the present moment be killed and usurped for a better moment in the future. Of course, this is dysfunctional because even if the future comes, it will come as the present moment, which is then usually again rejected out of hand for a new moment in the future.

Because thought is actually form, the spacious "nothingness" of the inner energy field of the body and the breath are its opposite. The compulsive focus on ideas of form keeps the vibration of the body's energy field at a lower, dense rate. This depletes your energy and makes you more prone to negative reactions and less-than-ideal outcomes. Further, someone who resonates at a chronic, lower energy field *attracts* others with the same low energy and myriad negative experiences. This is what happens in many seemingly random acts of violence: two similarly dense and thus "matching" pain bodies have become unconsciously attracted to each other.

The opposite matching also occurs: two people of relatively high vibrations also mutually attract. Such rare couples are an ideal match because the usual drama of pain-body-triggered chaos is absent. When two people do not unconsciously need each other to constantly provide negative nourishment for their pain bodies, real love is present. Otherwise, the more common love-hate dynamics predominate, which is little more than two active pain bodies feeding on arguments, and masquerading as romance.

The present moment is that thin slice of the now. It is just this moment, and is beautifully simple and elegantly accessible. The present moment is often confused with the *content* of the present moment, all the stuff that's happening.

*Circumstances that happen in the present moment are not the same thing as the present moment itself.*

The present moment is invisible. It is made of essence; it is the life force. The present moment is not a *thing or event*.

In the same way that the inner energy field of the body can be equated with stillness and is thus the present moment, the outer physical body is the form or matter that exists as something extraneous to this inner quality of stillness. The physical body is not of itself the stillness, which is why effective spiritual practice involves noticing the *inner* energy field of the body as a contrast to it. "Stuff" or circumstances are not the present moment. The peace alone that undergirds whatever shows up is what the present moment is.

Wild animals reside perfectly in the calm of the present moment. Even if their survival is threatened and they take flight with fast, focused action, they are not burdened with heavy emotional reactions. They are not worried about the past and do not compulsively plan and worry about the future. When hungry, they seek food, but it is done in the now. When another animal chases them and tries to kill them for dinner, the pursued may dash for its life, but it still does the dashing in the present moment of now.

It is a way of *being* that aligns with the true power of nature. This is the power of now described by Eckhart Tolle.

A common misconception about remaining calm in the present moment is that a person would not be able to rush in the face of a deadline, hurl out of the way of an on-coming truck, or race down a corridor to catch a plane. To the contrary, try it sometime. Simply move your body very fast. In fact, move it as fast as it will go; however, while doing this, focus on your breath and the inner energy field of the body and notice that you are still at peace, with a quiet mind, despite your sweating armpits. Of course, true mastery occurs when you race to catch a flight but remain unaffected when you miss it.

When you focus on the inner energy field of the body, or the breath, thoughts immediately subside and the power of now is accessed. This is why it is said that by virtue of accessing the first two gateways, the third is accessed automatically. Out of chaos, the essence of life shines through.

*Since every living creature is animated by an inner essence of stillness, the antidote to any problem or difficult person or individual suffering is to add more stillness. You are consciously adding more of what you already are.*

As you regularly apply the antidote to any kind of suffering, take heart. Know that the process of transformation is beautifully progressing in your life.

6

# Reclaiming Essence from Your Pain Body

UNTIL YOU WITNESS THE profound increase of your vital power as your inner essence becomes reclaimed from the pain body, you may not have recognized just how disabled you have been. As your life force becomes recovered, your physical and emotional well-being is immediately enhanced, but ultimately, there is a far greater benefit: spiritual wisdom.

When you are unable to sense the greater, broader *spiritual* perspective that underlies all events, circumstances, experiences, and relationships, you are like a mouse in a maze that cannot see beyond its walls to the vast and lovely world in which we live. This limited perspective is what drives most people's pursuit of meaninglessness and their focus on trivia. It *always* causes disruption and disharmony because it is minutia driven, not spiritually based. Focusing on minor nuances of anything having to do with matter, such as bodies, furniture, clothes, or the context in which they exist, is immature, spiritually speaking.

With this limited focus one misses the bigger picture: creating and sustaining an environment of deep peace and bliss for yourself and those around you. Spiritual insight is usually sorely lacking, although this lack is almost never recognized because you are still perceiving through the pain body's lens. You are in the maze but don't know that.

When you escape from the maze of minutia focus, you escape from the fixation on targeting *incorrect* areas for improvement or enhancement. Escapees readily recognize the paradox at work: you could not make this distinction while *in* the maze, and had to be freed to some degree to peek outside the box and recognize that an escape route even exists: the antidote. But when your life force is trapped by the pain body, you are stuck in the box. As you reclaim your vital energy, clarity and wisdom return as your birthright.

When you consider a recovery of all of your vital essence while still in the maze, you most likely don't fully recognize just how much of your vital energy is obscured. When operating at a third of your battery capacity for a long time, one becomes accustomed to less power. It is not until all circuits are fully charged that by contrast the sudden renewal feels like a total rebirth. This is not merely physical vitality as we normally consider it. The quadriplegic can emit extraordinary life force, whereas a stunt person may have more physical agility but less spiritual essence shining through.

This power is the potent essence of life that animates everything and wants to express itself through you, but cannot until it is freed up.

As you recover your essence, the material world will be affected, spiritually speaking, by your increased energetic fluctuations; however, it will also be affected in a literal sense, and this can serve to help you recognize when your fire's glow is expanding in scope.

Recently I drove with Jeannette from Los Angeles to San Francisco for her to see her extended family. On the long drive northbound, as is always the case, there was ample opportunity to align fully with my inner essence by focusing on the inner energy field of the body, by placing attention on the deep breaths, and by fully observing the spacious stillness that surrounds me. Under these circumstances, there was no way to *avoid* feeling absolutely rejuvenated upon my arrival at our hotel, seven hours later. By staying blissfully in the moment, without thoughts focusing on the past or future, the entire journey felt as though it took fifteen minutes. In fact, the sense of deep pleasure that was present at journey's end was not simply a *feeling* of well-being, but there was also an expansion of life force, an almost explosive inner energetic surge that could melt ice. This is an important point because if *you* do not experience regular, explosive surges of your own inner force, then where is it being used? Energy cannot be destroyed. So if *you* are not benefitting from it, who is? Your power is there somewhere, but where?

Someone or something is definitely benefitting by all that natural life force, but it's not *you*. It's the pain body with all of its counterproductive, life-denying strategies and goals. The pain body is the very entity that has been siphoning your inner essence for its own purposes, like an energy vampire. If you've ever experienced another's or your own explosive rage; or it has turned inward into long-term depression or mood swings, then you know that there is indeed an inner fire present. That inner fire, when co-opted by the pain body, erupts into anger and rage at others or self, rather than one that compassionately flowers into a deep abiding connection with everyone.

This profound recapturing of your vital force, as was mentioned previously, can affect your physical environment. Although this is not at all meaningful in and of itself, it is vitally important as an *indicator* of just how weak your voltage has been up to this point. When it comes flowing back to you, you'll notice it—and so will appliances and electronic devices. You can watch for this to occur, not as a way to gain egoic satisfaction and to feel special, but rather, as an indicator that your fire is now indeed burning more brightly. Even so, your own deepening peace and calm will have already indicated that this is the case.

Enlightenment is not a *special* state. To the contrary, it is your *natural* state, and one that is inevitably reclaimed as you progress in your spiritual growth. It is not in question as to whether or not each person's awakening is underway. That is guaranteed. The only question has to do with efficiency. How much suffering is necessary before you will more *consciously*—and thus more efficiently—participate in the process as you uncover your self-realized state?

*Once the opening toward self-realization is efficiently underway, the process necessarily involves stepping out of agreement with the material world.*

When this happens, your electromagnetic frequency changes. This is the basis for enlightenment itself because you re-align with your inherent connection with source and leave your previous identification with "things" behind. As such, your new vibration is of a vastly faster vibration than is the world of things. "Things" belong to the world of matter that was manufactured within a framework of a particular dense energetic atmosphere; form or things are made by other things (machines) operated by humans who are not yet awakened, and thus all of that has a certain dense vibration. The widget next to you is literally in the world that made it, but you are evolving out of it. So, when *you,* now awakened, meet *it,* sparks fly. This "meeting" is not magical or mysterious, or even rare. You have simply disrobed from the extraneous layers that obscured your essence, and now you stand shining and bright. All that has been manufactured and that surrounds you is of the previous era, and *it* has some adjusting to do, in a manner of speaking. Your vibrational impact on it does not make you a circus act, or even an anomaly. The current paradigm of things will also necessarily shift, as it falls in line behind *you,* the new human. In a very real sense, *everything* is transforming.

We, as so-called modern humans, are at a singularly unique point along the evolutionary track, awakening in the midst of this current modern electronic world. Jesus and the Buddha awakened in a virtual wilderness, comparatively speaking. The trees and the deer that surrounded *them,* no doubt also shifted in response to their arising essence, but the chasm between their material world—their clay pots and them—*then*, and our information age—our electronics and us—*now*, is incomprehensibly greater. As a result, our electronic existence will be newly experiencing *you.*

As Jeannette and I completed our drive to San Francisco and arrived at our hotel, a new environment for me, the electrical front door of the lobby immediately broke, the magnetic key pad at our room door had to be disassembled and repaired, the wall heater in the room went out, and my cell phone was affected. Later, at her relatives' home, the heat mechanism on the clothes dryer that I was using stopped working and my laptop became completely inoperable. Our arrival created four separate repair visits by the hotel engineer. This becomes a relatively predictable experience for any being who is recovering the full capacity of their life force. A new era is here, and the awakening human heralds it through their arising and increasing force field. This should not come as a surprise to you or even seem strange, given that caterpillars can turn into butterflies and tadpoles into frogs, and when they do, they move into expanded habitats. From the ground to the air and from the water to land, transforming creatures move into new habitats to accommodate their evolution. Humans are transforming radically, and along with that shift, our entire physical world has an opportunity to shift with us as it accommodates the new human, *here*. As you witness certain changes with the material objects around you as your energy is reclaimed, give thanks. Joyfully, the movement toward wholeness leaves out nothing.

Because each human being, when aligned with space consciousness, can finally be the true and vital instrument through which the life force flows unheeded, you become a virtual powerhouse of electromagnetic surge more fully capable of creation. But it is not you who is creating; it is the dynamic force of life that surges *through you*.

*I can of mine own self do nothing.*

This life force or essence can finally flow through *you* fully as an instrument for peace through all its differing creative manifestations. And this is where spiritual wisdom comes into play, because once freed somewhat from the limited perspective of the maze, you have increased clarity and wisdom to *appropriately* take effective action in all the areas of your life. You will know what changes or corrections are needed, if any, and they may be very different from the ones that you would have made while blinded by your mouse perspective: changes can be implemented to benefit your family, profession, and physical health. Finally you will be able to put into effect global changes because you have gained the only thing that can help all of it: spiritual maturity.

When you reclaim your lost essence, you are not adding something new. You are not adding more life essence, but rather you are uncovering the essence that is already there but is obscured. As was stated previously, it is difficult to use language to describe the essence of life because it is nothing, a "no-thing." Essence is invisible and pure. Since words and language are comprised of actual matter or form, you can see the challenge in using matter to describe "something" that has *no* matter. It's challenging to describe something that is "nothing." So, if you want to uncover a being's true essence in order to soothe and heal, then words and language would not be an ideal healing balm, unless the speaker is rooted in being through the use of the three gateways.

Words and language can still be used, but they only have healing properties if the transmitter of the words and language is imbued with this same palpable essence, or is able to create space and tap into their essence. Again, the essence is already present, but usually it's covered up. So it's essential for any transmitter of healing, whether they are a parent, a caregiver of an Alzheimer's patient, a massage therapist, a partner, or a lover, to be radiating at full "battery" or "essence" capacity.

Many, but not all, late-stage Alzheimer's patients embody an almost complete absence of useable essence, like a car battery that needs a full charge. As is the case for anyone who is in an active temper tantrum or angry outburst, the pain body seeks to remain active and so compulsively searches for drama to sustain it and hide its essence. Most people do not recognize this drama for what it is, but confuse another's temper tantrum as a need for love. At its core, this is true, but adding love does not mean adding drama. Agreeing to engage the pain body's addiction for the drama is not providing love; it's strengthening the pain body, which wants to chronically disrupt and create upset.

No pain body can ever be satisfied and will always find a new problem to blame for its unhappiness. This is why attempting to appease unhappiness is a hopeless proposition because the pain body's source of misery is a bottomless pit. No amount of talk therapy will satisfy its addiction to discontent unless the pain body's density is targeted for dissolving. Of course, the pain body relishes reflection on one's own or others' past hurts, failures, successes, or perceived problems, and will talk about them end-lessly to a therapist or caregiver. Or, it will talk about gaining some goal or object in the future which will make it happy. When you attempt to point this out to a person who is at the mercy of a dense and frequently active pain body, it may be possible to crack their defensive shell, if they begin to suspect that no matter what solution is offered, misery is just around the corner.

Often, one partner in a relationship can spend the entire span of the relationship attempting to make their partner "happy," to no avail. This is futile since the partner whose pain body is active has no intention of surrendering its status as manipulator in charge. The pain body is the perfect bully. It is a master at holding the entire schoolyard, household, or work environment hostage.

Attempting to bargain with an active pain body by giving it what it wants is tantamount to bargaining with a terrorist hold-ing a gun to a hostage's head. The pain body demands attention in the precise way that a spoiled adolescent does through dys-functional means. It will do anything in order to gain acknowl-edgment that it, the pain body, is suffering terribly and thereby deserves the utmost attention by demanding that you also agree that problems abound. It will do this dance despite others' need for harmony. In fact, when it suspects that peace has found a momentary inroad into the environment, or especially when it detects the slightest hint of inner peace arising in the partner, it will redouble its efforts. No household or environment can enjoy more than momentary snippets of peace until an active pain body is targeted for dissolving; or one of the partners becomes grounded in presence and refuses to be pulled into the dance in which the pain body creates a daily laundry list of items needing correction. Absent from the list is its own instigative role in famil-ial or group disharmony.

The most effective way to handle an active pain body is to

absolutely refuse to engage in its dance and to instead assist the other to notice that, no matter what apparent problem is corrected, more will be found. There is very little discussion, unless you are aligned with presence, that will not feed an active pain body that insists on your capitulation to its dire assessments of imperfection. So keep the exchange gently simple and direct, as though talking to an angry three-year-old. It is best to simply restate over and over that everything is okay, and whatever steps need to be taken to improve something will be done when appropriate. But the greatest improvement of all will occur only when both partners' pain bodies are targeted for dissolving. Otherwise, you chase phantom problems into eternity and no happiness will ever be attained.

Once the goal of becoming aware of and thus reducing the pain body's control and dominance is mutually agreed upon, then and only then can true and lasting change be implemented. Once you both agree that no one person's dense pain body will be allowed to manage the family, peace becomes the sponsor of change and this will make a world of difference. Of course, strategies and corrections can be noticed and implemented, but not as dictated to by the pain body, which by its nature is not capable of being satisfied.

Of course, this response and perspective will not satisfy the pain body, and it will accelerate its demand to draw you in; however, align firmly with stillness by accessing any of the three gateways. Immediately take several deep, long breaths, and allow them to "take" you to the inner energy field of the body, to your essence.

Observe the pain body and how it has taken over your beloved. Recall how you, too, may have reacted similarly. Notice the heavy, dense vibration of it. Can you feel how uncomfortable its energy is? At once deeply pleasurable like an addict's fix, pain body flare-ups also have a flip side: they create a deeper pain, which cannot be resolved.

Attempting to appease the pain body, by engaging with it in its demand for attention, bolsters it and reinforces this pattern more firmly for the next time it emerges to feed. Appeasing it by engaging in conflict or agreeing to minutia-focus may work momentarily, but, over the long term, a higher order of handling must be introduced. When the pain body has pulled an emotional response out of you, it will predictably return within minutes or hours for yet more drama on which to feed. If you have reacted negatively, immediately place your focus on the inner energy field of the body and the breath, and you will align again with presence. The effectiveness of the three gateways cannot be overstated, particularly when you're in an emergency situation. When someone in your midst erupts, immediately turn inward and align with essence in this way. Not only will you benefit, but your essence will flow into them, and thus, they are also healed.

Even when it appears that your partner or family member is not interested in growing spiritually, by your example, they cannot help but to grow and expand along with you. Although in some cases, a partner with a very dense pain body will simply leave a relationship because its pain body cannot tolerate much peace, many other relationships are transformed, even when just one person becomes more conscious. Your own example in aligning with stillness and the consequent peace that ensues will provide more leadership, and thus healing, than any other single factor.

Within the context of a conscious relationship, both partners can agree beforehand that the person whose pain body has not been activated becomes the "designated driver," so to speak. This is another irritation for the pain body, which always demands that it alone is the master of the house and possesses the sole criterion for right discernment in all areas. As such, the designated driver will never be accepted by an active pain body and so these arrangements must be made prior to a flare-up.

The designated driver then holds stillness for both parties during an "eruption," until the other person's essence has been reclaimed and they regain their sanity. At a later time, spiritual practice can be reintroduced to address each other's pain-body reactions. Of course, when the DP has an irreversible brain disease, which does not allow conscious steps to be introduced, the spouse, the caregiver, or the family member must alone hold the space of consciousness or essence on behalf of the afflicted person. In fact, anyone in the presence of someone emotionally out of control automatically becomes the designated driver and must immediately access one of the three gateways to prevent their pain body from being pulled into the drama. Naturally, the person whose pain body is inactive will be making this distinction alone, since the other person will not easily concede to sharing any authority or power.

There are times when the active pain body is in full force, and it seems that if you attempt to reason with it, this will encourage the pain body to retreat, but this is incorrect. Any words spoken to a person whose pain body is active must be sourced from stillness. Be quiet and allow the essence of life to speak through you, if you speak at all. Sometimes such words, often used with questions of inquiry, cut straight through the pain body's defenses and you can actually see the other's compulsive thinking stop. Once after entering a bookstore with Jeannette, she immediately purchased something and then turned to leave, demanding that I fall in line and follow. Her impatience is consistent with her general need to keep rushing toward a different and better future moment; even though, just as soon as it arrives, she is equally unhappy with it. As Jeannette stood near the door, angry hands on hips, purchase in hand, I asked her firmly but gently, "Where are we rushing to?" Doing this while fully grounded in presence, my eyes met hers, and her physical body actually froze as her mind stopped completely. She stared at me, as though momentarily in disbelief at having her mind stopped in its tracks. The bookstore owner, standing with us, asked me, "How did you *do* that?" She was referring to the ability of essence to cut through the chaos of the mind and invite it to stop, which only occurs when mind is confronted with presence, not more mental noise.

Had I attempted to stall Jeannette through coercion or manipulative flattery, or by attempting to reason with her pain body, it would actually solidify and encourage future outbreaks. It may retreat momentarily but emerges again that much quicker. Acts of supplication, by taking an inferior stance in order to plead with the pain body, is itself a negative emotional reaction and virtually invites its dance and it grows in momentum. Instead, add presence by taking a deep breath and focusing on the "in and out" of your breathing. You thus align with presence, and there is no way to know how the essence of life will use or speak through you. Be open to the source of all life healing the moment in a new and fresh way. You may be surprised that your true essence will initiate an inroad for change that had not previously been considered or known by you.

Breathe deeply; immediately place your attention on the inner energy field of the body. Observe how your thoughts immediately slow down and the effect this has on you and your DP. By applying the antidote of presence, both the conscious as well as the unconscious person are soothed—at least until the pain body reappears for its next feeding. Over time, however, adding presence creates an opening for spiritual growth and healing becomes possible in the DP, and will even lessen the pain body in the mentally afflicted.

When one of the partners becomes more firmly rooted in

presence, she can then help the other partner to dissolve his pain body as well. Then, both parties together can make their relationship a conscious one and together jointly dissolve their pain bodies and that of their children, which will bring lasting peace. Relating or making love essence to essence, rather than limiting physical togetherness to the meeting of body parts, is a remarkable experience, the basis of the Tantric Yoga tradition in the East.

An active pain body is most satisfied if it can pull your pain body into its active state. This is helpful to know if you are a caregiver or a partner to a DP, or if you have young children or teenagers. When two pain bodies become active together, the most dramatic display of emotions feed and accelerate each other. Unfortunately, each pain body then becomes reinforced and is that much stronger for its next feeding. This knowledge provides a context in which a caregiver, family member, parent, or partner can engage in effective spiritual practice and make it applicable within a difficult environment.

If someone in your presence erupts into anger, irritation, upset, or accusation, first recognize immediately that their pain body has been triggered and has emerged to feed on *your* pain body's reaction. A person may indeed feel anger or sadness without having their pain body triggered, but it is a temporary ripple on the ocean of experience and does not take over the person. To the contrary, an active pain body's anger is characterized by an attempt to right a wrong that was done to it or to someone else whom it perceives to be under its protection.

Sometimes you may have prior indication that another's pain body is gearing up to attack you, so be sure to take that opportunity to focus on your deep breathing and the inner energy field of the body. Do not respond at all verbally until you are aligned with peace, even if that means physically removing yourself to another room until you are conscious and aligned with presence.

You can do this anywhere, in your home or in a public place. Since your pain body needs you to express its demands or angry response, do not allow it to co-opt you. We don't generally recognize that our own mouth is actually under our own control and not our pain body's, although regularly the pain body will attempt to take over yours. If you refuse to open your mouth in order for a typical irritated or angry pain body response to be emitted, then it cannot use you in this way. If the other person demands your response, but you are not yet ready, simply pause first and take deep, slow breaths without saying anything. And then, once collected, say, "One moment, I'm considering what you are saying." This technique can be used during any difficult exchange within interpersonal or professional relationships. In fact, within an awakened person, their verbal responses are often delayed because they acquiesce to the voice of life speaking and acting through them. As such, the awakened person becomes sensitive to the desires of the essence of life and becomes empty so that the source can be expressed through them. There is no rush to respond or to act. An empty mind is the only true discerner of right words and action.

When you consider that you may be the only anchor to sanity within your family or group, guard peace as the sentinel that you are. But you as sentinel are effective through your alignment with peace, and nothing else, as this is the only effective healer.

Obviously, the most effective response to the pain body's disruptive cycles is to refrain from allowing it to pull yours into confrontation or even into a "noisy mind" discussion or debate. When this happens, you will recognize how unpleasant it feels, how you feel drained or that your life energy feels "sucked out." This is truer than you may realize because the very low, dense energy vibration of the pain body soaks up your essence and obscures it. The antidote is to add more "space" through use of the three gateways. The moment you begin to feel uncomfortable, focus again on your breath and the inner energy field of the body and keep returning to it if you have allowed your focus to drift.

In the event that you can feel your own pain body being triggered, simply observe its attempts to take *you* over. See if you can "catch" it before it takes you over completely and pretends to be you. Immediately focus on your breath and follow your breath deep inside, to the inner energy field of the body and your essence. Hold fast and don't be diverted by the strong pull of your own noisy mind that tells you to abandon such practices. The pain body wants you to get lost in drama. Don't allow it to manipulate your resolve to dissolve it.

Even if it is successful in taking you over, hold back some part of your attention and continue to observe how it gets pulled into the drama and engages. In other words, watch from afar so to speak, as you observe yourself argue or turn nasty yourself. Notice how the pain body becomes rigid in its view of events. It clings righteously to cherished opinions. Notice how your pain body, although pretending to dislike disharmony, actually feeds on it.

It is important to remember that the pain body is not *you,* any more than the other person's pain body is *him or her.* Realize this and refrain from making your pain body into an "identity" that you begin to believe is you. It's just the pain body that *pretends* to be you. And through effective spiritual practice, it can be dissolved. Remember, you—and all others—are comprised of life essence, not emotional baggage.

After a dense pain body has emerged to feed, strewing drama through yelling, crying, moaning, and complaining, and has been fed, it will retreat and the person returns with smiles and finally feels satisfied and "happy." This is precisely the time when one partner can initiate conversation with the other partner about their mutually active pain bodies, and together they can consciously take steps to reduce them. This is also when a parent can speak to their child, after he has calmed down and the tantrum has passed. This suggests that during an active pain body cycle, it is not productive to attempt to point out that "your pain body is active and you're out of control." Because the pain body has taken over the being, don't expect it to gently agree that it's a demon. Instead, it will no doubt counter that it is *your* pain body that is active and feeding. Indeed, if you or someone else becomes indignant or angry, it is evident that the pain body is speaking and is now using your newfound awareness to bolster itself. Since the pain body knows no limits in its cunning and scope, naturally it will adopt a new identity of "spiritual practitioner" and self-righteously point out evidence of *your* pain body's existence. For this reason, always limit dialogue about this subject to those times when both parties are calm and relatively free of anger and irritation.

Instead, first access the three gateways yourself and get yourself well grounded in being and essence. Next, you may *gently* suggest to your partner that he "take a few deep breaths and focus on the inner energy field of the body." If your partner is already familiar with this practice and follows your advice, he may recover and recognize that indeed his pain body may be active, but for this to happen there must already be a sufficient degree of spiritual intimacy and trust established between you. The difference is that you are not eliciting the other's defense mechanisms as strongly by "calling out" the pain body to itself.

Whether fully active or not, no pain body will ever take steps that will orchestrate its own undoing. In the same way that you would not expect spiritual maturity and wisdom from a drunken man, do not expect spiritual maturity or self-awareness from an active pain body. Simply ride out the outbreak, wait for the inner being to return, and then initiate a conversation about how to limit future drama by bringing awareness to the pain body's actual need for conflict that has not yet been recognized.

Of course, responding calmly while another's pain body is active takes spiritual maturity because the normal routine is for one person to become "active" and attack the other person; and then, the second person is triggered and his/her pain body becomes active too. Then, you're off to the dance, the pain body waltz.

If you have been affected by an active pain body, it's natural to seek out stillness or nature in order to regain some level of presence. Because your presence has become further "encased" by the pain body, effective spiritual practice actually recaptures this lost presence or essence. When affected by an active pain body, a quiet environment is also helpful to regain a sense of peace. Since space is the same thing as stillness, or pure life force, you may instinctively retreat to the outdoors or the quiet of a back bedroom in order to regain equanimity. You may not necessarily recognize that your presence has been polluted with dense energy and it feels dreadful. Unless the pain body is dissolved through effective spiritual practice, it will emerge to feed in relatively the same pattern, over and over and over again. We all know when two people's active pain bodies engage, year in and year out, and it is called a dysfunctional relationship.

By focusing your attention on the breath and the inner energy field of the body, it is indeed possible to hold fast to presence and *not* be pulled into drama. You can listen in a state of alert awareness as the other is yelling, criticizing, or verbally attacking. The other's pain body won't like it, of that you can be sure, and it will increase the volume of its drama or adopt a different tactic altogether in order to insure that you *do* react; however, remain grounded in being and rooted in essence until the storm passes.

When you have achieved this level of mastery, during which

you can remain perfectly at peace, focusing on your deep breathing and the inner energy field of the body at the same time that you are being provoked and verbally attacked, you are in an enlightened state.

Sometimes, the other's active pain body, out of frustration at not eliciting a reaction from you, will simply pick something up and throw it across the room or will break or pound on something. Then, if you negatively react to the broken object, the pain body has now drawn you in after all. The pain body will notice that this strategy is effective, and you can be certain that it will try it again next time. This is not to say that you cannot respond calmly with a high quality, but firm, "No!" but do not react negatively, and especially, do not allow this demonstration to seduce you into showering additional negative attention on the person. If you engage with it, the pain body waltz is in effect and all the rules apply relative to addictions, so don't be surprised that agreements, promises, or sound reasoning do not hold up. Instead, become the silent witness and adopt a stance of alert awareness. Definitely leave the room immediately, but calmly, if you must, demonstrating your disinterest and refusal to get drawn in further. This is when you can invite the other person to take a break, to take a few deep breaths, and allow them to get a bit of "space" in order to calm down; however, take care not to cross the line into "stonewalling" or punishing the other person when their pain body is active. You are simply holding a place of alert awareness with compassion because you only too well remember when your own active pain body was so invoked.

Over time, through the use of effective spiritual practice, you are able to dissolve your pain body, and its stored energy is recaptured for use by you. As you get more practiced in refusing to engage with another's pain body, you will notice that the force behind both pain bodies lessens, rather than strengthens. You are helping another, as well as you, to reclaim your essence and hope-fully find this ecstasy more satisfying than the enervating and shallow pleasure of the pain body's addictive cycle.

It is always more effective, and ultimately the healthiest and most sane response, to meet the fury of an awakened pain body with an alert awareness. This means that you simply look, with-out judgment or comment. There need be no response at all. This alert awareness is presence, the state of quiet mind that is the only singularly effective remedy against problematic people and situa-tions. The way to achieve a state of alert awareness is by accessing any of the three gateways. Then, words or conversation can be added to the equation, but they must speak to the essence of the person to have any real benefit, *not* the egoic mind structure and the pain body.

In the case of declining cognitive ability in Alzheimer's or dementia patients, or even when responding to the fury of a two-year-old child's awakening pain body, you can still use simple yet effective conversation that invites the other person to observe that in actual fact, he is okay. The pain body screams its demands that you immediately make a change, correction, or adjustment on its behalf right now, in order to "save" it from some imagined problem or disaster. But just because the intensity of the demand is great doesn't mean you have to agree that there is anything at all wrong or that any response on your part is needed. You, rather than the pain body, must set the peaceful tone of the moment and stay in a state of alert awareness. Immediately access the three gateways. Become fully rooted in your own being before attempting to navi-gate a DP's pain body. Because it insists that there is a catastrophe happening "out there" causing its suffering, it is imperative that you first fully align with your essence in order to assist the DP in recognizing that their own upset is an illusion of the highest order to prove that the world is unsafe. When a DP reacts in this manner, you are simply witnessing an active pain body coming out to feed and looking for problems to create a drama.

If there is a "catastrophe," it's an inner not an outer one. Whether active within an adult or a child, the turmoil and suffering is indeed present, but it is inside them, caused by mental objection to the present moment. So, when an active pain body emerges and points out that there is a catastrophe occurring, do *not* agree that whatever is pointed out in that moment is actually a catastrophe. This may sound obvious, but too often you unconsciously agree with the pain body's version of the cause of its suffering. When this happens, the dance begins and you are now both off to join in the pain body waltz.

When a DP's or child's pain body emerges, you may be tempted to ask, "Why are you so upset?" Of course, you may be caught off guard by the force behind the pain body's anger or upset over some minor setback or circumstance. But if you ask why they are upset, you are actually speaking to the "monster" who has taken over, rather than the person whose true inner essence has been usurped. For this reason, you will not receive a mature, honest, or even predictable response. All that will be elicited is an entry point for the pain body to pull you in to the "reality" of its nightmare. You will know the real reason behind its reaction: it's a pain body. It gets offended. It likes to create havoc; that's what it does. So don't engage with it. Don't negotiate with a terrorist. Simply hold fast to consciousness by immediately placing attention on the inner energy field of the body and taking deep breaths; keep a stance of alert awareness until the storm passes. When responding to a child, you can still address their immediate needs or concerns, but you do so without agreeing that their drama or upset is necessary or normal in any way.

If you must respond verbally at all, keep it short. Do not look into the eyes of an active pain body because doing so will more easily trigger yours. In fact, you may notice that when you refuse to make eye contact that it will demand it. Interesting, isn't it? The pain body knows that its energy is contagious. Eye contact can indeed pull you right in to the dance of the pain body, no matter your best intention; however, once enlightened, pain bodies or negative energy fields won't affect you at all.

When a DP confronts you, simply look away and calmly and gently, with slow speech, point out that everything will be okay. You can even focus your attention in the direction of the other person's face, but not actually look into their eyes, and they will probably not notice. When you respond, you can state that the (imagined) source of the problem has no power to hurt or cause upset. Of course, the active pain body will be infuriated by this nonreaction and will demand that you see things as it does. It wants you to see and pay homage to *it*. But that's all right. Just continue to stay calm and alert, and remind their inner being, who is obscured during this outbreak, that it is safe, loved, and cared for—at least in this moment—and that the thing "over there" is only an apparent problem but has no real power to disrupt. Then, you as the spouse, parent, or caregiver can simultaneously consider if there is any correction needed regarding the supposed source of upset, but refuse to agree that the problem is of any magnitude.

To the onlooker, the scene may be surprising inasmuch as the "objective" caregiver, parent, or partner may appear to be too detached or uncaring, but upon closer inspection, you will observe a calm refusal to join in the dance of the pain body. Ultimately, this ensures a healing response, rather than further feeding it with an emotional reaction in an attempt to appease the monster of the pain body by allowing it to hold you hostage by fearing its reactions.

Any slight reduction in a pain body's density is a permanent one. Helping each other and your children to reduce the fury and neediness of the pain body is the greatest gift you can bestow upon another, because these gains are not lost as the person ages and ultimately faces death. A dissolving pain body, having allowed the light of essence to finally shine through, allows it to better deal with change of all kinds. Remember this when you feel you are helping an active pain body by allowing it to manipulate you and draw you in to its dance, when instead you are unconsciously strengthening it. Love the other person enough by refusing to allow their pain body to use you to both your detriment.

Allowing an active pain body to use you by engaging with it is not love, although it is often confused as such. While most recognize the extreme shifts in mood inherent with Alzheimer's disease, almost everyone's personality goes back and forth daily with similar if less intense moods and outbursts. But make no mistake: the pain body is the demon causing the problem, no matter the diagnosis or the individual who is upset. With respect to Alzheimer's disease, although there is an underlying neurological impairment, preceding its advancement—or precipitating it as some spiritual practitioners do believe—was a pain body looking to overthrow its host.

If you are able to effectively handle the active pain body of any DP by aligning with presence, you will have achieved a level of mastery that will serve you in healing a moderate or dense pain body within any interpersonal relationship or setting. The way to align with presence is by accessing any of the three gateways. Ultimately, though, responsibility to fully observe your *own* pain body and thus take steps to dissolve it is of utmost importance.

Almost everyone without exception, until a spiritual awakening occurs, is either hurting physically from an illness or injury, or they are in pain emotionally and mentally to some degree. Suffering, whether emotional or physical, seems to be prevalent.

Hence, most everyone is a sucker for a quick cure. We need and want instant relief.

Although most people are not aware of it, the ultimate state of spiritual awakening—enlightenment—is the end to suffering as we commonly know it. Because the enlightened person has dis-identified with the mind's activity, suffering is almost impossible for any sustained period. Enlightenment and suffering are opposites. A self-realized person can still feel anger or can grieve personal loss, but such anger or grief is very short-lived and does not permeate deeply as it does for other people and does not feed a pain body.

It would seem that the enlightened person has somehow stumbled upon a magical elixir that heals all hurt. At long last, there really is an ultimate application or practice, which when applied, produces immediate benefits. But unlike over-the-counter fixes, this one's free.

Once the obstacle to awakening is identified—the objections by the mind to a spiritual practice—the antidote is applied quite easily. An antidote that dissolves mental suffering, no matter the cause of that suffering.

*Remember, the mind doesn't actually want you to end mental suffering.*

Remaining in the now and thus at peace, through use of these practices, is very upsetting to the mind. It would be much happier if you were unhappy and worried.

But now you have the opportunity to leave behind the familiar maze of mental suffering and strife and accept your initiation to the realms of soaring flight, free from the entanglements of the pain body. If you are reading these words, your own pain body must be in the dormant state, so read quickly before it emerges to feed and throws this book in the trash.

# 7

## Identification with Roles, Forms, and Attributes

Up to this point, we have been exploring the way that chronic mental thought convinces *you* that there is some problem over there with this or that, with this person or that person—some problem that you need to fix, straighten, solve, or orchestrate *right now*. Chronic thought has *you* identifying with its concerns; but this is not the only way that it operates within you. In addition to convincing you that every thought is true, accurate, and *vital*, the egoic mind strongly *aligns* with outside "things" as part of its false identity.

In truth, *you* are none of these things. *You* are an invisible essence; *you* share the same vital life force that makes up everything. So why does the mind want you to take on a strong identification with "things" that are fleeting and subject to constant change and dissolution—when you are really everlasting and permanent by your very nature? Because this causes you extreme anxiety and deep inner conflict, which further distances you from your essence and has you returning again to chronic mental activity.

The way that this conflict is attempted to be resolved, on an unconscious level, is to simply add more "things" outside of you with which to identify. In the same way that an addict may, to some degree, recognize his own addictive patterns, that very recognition causes anxiety, which leads to further substance abuse in order to handle the underlying anxiety. It becomes a vicious cycle.

This type of mental pattern sets up a deeper inner conflict inside you because, at your essence, you *know* who you are. You can sense the truth of it; but your mind is a cunning hypnotist and convinces you that you are *it and its false identifications*, which are fleeting and subject to dissolution. Because this is the nature of the mind, but not of *you*, it tries to convince you that you are like *it*. Because it's running the show in your life, you unwittingly continue to allow it to set the pace, set the standard, and set the *context* by which you live.

In addition to keeping you in avoidance of the present moment, the egoic thought structure also convinces you that certain roles that you play, certain things that you own, and certain attributes that you are endowed with are vitally essential for your survival and are, in effect, the actual *you*.

This is similar to a child who grows up believing that she has been born to particular parents, in a particular city, only to discover later that she was adopted. Her entire life was spent identifying her parents as her parents, and when she discovers that they were her surrogates, she develops an identity crisis. The mind, determined to find an attachment, is deeply offended when its attachments get derailed and so will go searching for another one that it feels is more suitable. It is also instructive in this case to see how the mind is in a chronic state of searching for evidence of its stability and of a deeper connection to self. In fact, there is no role, attribute, or form that can provide this sense of meaning or sense of self, nor can *any* of them ever really be *yours*. In the deepest sense, they are *not* required for survival, and in fact false attachments to roles, forms, and attributes diminish your survivability. When your essence is obscured by mental hypnosis such as described here, your quality of living is reduced because mental suffering predominates.

In addition to accessing the stillness of the present moment by using the three gateways, there is an additional spiritual practice that helps to dissolve egocentric ideas about who you really are. The process to full ripeness, spiritually speaking, requires a softening of identifications with roles, forms, and attributes. Like the peach that is fully ripened, the outer hardness of your egoic shell must soften until the sweetness of your true essence shines through.

What I mean by "identification" is the practice of regarding something that is *not* you as though it *is* you. When you consciously or unconsciously conceive of a role, attribute, or form (things of matter) as virtually *part* of you, then you are identified with it. You believe that this other thing *is* you.

Three primary areas of misidentification are to that of roles, forms, and attributes.

A "role" is a characteristic and expected social behavior of an individual—a function or position. Sometimes, your roles are so deeply ingrained that you wouldn't be able to recognize yourself without them.

When I speak of "form," I am referring to anything that is generally comprised of matter: your car or house, wardrobe, lawnmower, husband or wife, paycheck, or job title. As dysfunctional as it is, while being completely normal, most everyone fully identifies some pile of metal, wood, glass, or gristle, as *them*. They believe that their car, vacation home, or physical beauty defines the deepest part of them, and when it or part of it is lost through any means, it feels as if more than just a thing has gone. It's as though a part of *you* went with it.

An "attribute" is a quality or characteristic inherent in or ascribed to someone or something. For example, if you are a professional piano player and have a deeply ingrained identification with your ability to play a piano, what happens if you lose or damage your hand? Suddenly, you are no longer able to demonstrate your musical finesse. One of your ingrained attributes, "superb musical talent," suddenly dissolves and then you suffer from its loss.

This is also the case for a woman who has been considered to be beautiful her entire life. But as she ages and loses that physical attribute, intense suffering results because she so strongly identified herself as a beautiful woman.

Identifications sometimes cross one into the other. For example, in the example of the pianist, he has an "attribute" of being musically talented, but also there is the strong "role" of piano player that he identifies with. In this case, it doesn't matter in which category the identification falls. The power lies in becoming aware that, indeed, multiple identifications *exist* to your spiritual detriment.

## Identifying Identifications

The following spiritual practice was developed by me and successfully implemented prior to my awakening, so I know how powerful the process can be. It is comprised of two parts: First, it requires a brutally objective assessment of the roles, forms, and attributes that your ego uses to make itself feel important. Then, once those are identified, you reflect on each entry individually and imagine that it has suddenly vanished. This requires quiet reflection or meditation in order to fully access the spark of imagination that allows it to become real for you. Once dissolved in your imagination, your actual and true worth as pure life essence can be realized, and then put into context in your everyday experience.

This is the kind of spiritual practice that few seekers actually apply to any depth because the result of its application causes the entire egoic mind structure to stiffen in alarm. If bravery is mustered, and the practice is continued and held in awareness as you maneuver throughout daily life, a powerful reorientation occurs with respect to *correct* "self-identification." This is the true meaning of "self-realization." You are gradually recognizing your *true* self, until all your previous, mistaken identities fall away like old skin.

In the process of implementing this spiritual practice, you can hardly avoid discomfort in dismantling the ego's counterfeit self-importance. Although this practice has its particular challenges, once fully embraced, you will soon look back on any discomfort and chuckle at this false phantom. At first glance, the exercise may seem inappropriate and counterproductive. Well, you are partially correct, because this is what your mind is telling you. The essence of *you,* your true "being-ness," is not at all concerned with upholding a false image or creating a marketable enterprise out of you. The need to accumulate saleable images and the habit of fearing an unknown future are synonymous with the mind's activity. *You*—the stillness of you—is already vibrantly alive and animates your body and mind. *You,* believe it or not, need very little stuff for lasting well-being.

*You* do not fear aging, death, taxes, or your children's failure. *You* are aligned with the same life essence that imbues the clouds, ocean, and stars. *You* are made up of all the same "stuff," and this lovely essence cannot be distinguished from the essence of a shooting star or pristine white lily.

Consequently, in order to unravel *you* from the knot of everything and every role that you are *not* and bring you to peace, you must become aware of where you hold too tightly to ingrained roles, forms, and attributes—your *false* identities. Although it is understood that, heretofore, you have probably assumed that these are positive identities or enhancements, not false ones. But whatever extraneous layers added to the simplicity and perfection of *you,* has been added by the egoic thought structure, *not by you.*

This exercise emerged intuitively, as I more deeply came to recognize what stood in the way of my own enlightenment. Without this particular aspect of my spiritual practice, it is doubtful that I could have awakened. It can assist you in developing an ongoing *sensitivity of perception* that asks you to *notice* how you strongly identify with things that aren't even *you.* Until this process has been completed, you can't *get* to you; you can't uncover yourself from the thick blanket of falsehood that pretends to *be* you.

So let's begin the exercise wherein you will make a list of all those roles, forms, and attributes that you determine make up your image of yourself.

Divide a piece of paper into three columns and add one heading to each: Roles, Forms, and Attributes. Then, begin to identify what those entries would be when considering all roles, forms, and attributes that if lost, would readily create intense suffering. To clarify, simply brainstorm with paper and pen all the things (roles, forms, and attributes) that you have determined you cannot live without.

Note those entries that you feel really make up all your identifications, which are actually quite false, comprising the "little me"—the ego. It's the part of you that whines for trivialities and complains about people. It's the part of you that has you convinced that these "things" are necessary for your happiness, image, security, safety, health, or survival. Hence, this list is made from observing the ego's perspective in identifying *its* needs and wants; however, the fact that it's really the list of the ego's own makeup cannot usually be discerned yet. This distinction takes a certain degree of spiritual maturity to comprehend, and is in fact the maturity that is being developed here. For now, simply fill in the columns on your list, as you normally operate from your usual mental patterns.

For example, when Jeannette lost the ability to drive, she suffered miserably because she had so fully identified with her role as a driver but also, with that of "form," her automobile. This role and this form virtually *defined* her, in her own mind. It didn't matter to her that she had me as a chauffeur, whenever she needed one, so the argument about losing her freedom didn't hold up. Even when it was pointed out that an ever-present chauffer could actually enhance her life, it was dismissed out of hand. There was virtually no ability to place this change of circumstances in any other context than an abject loss. In her case, because there was really no inherent suffering in losing her license and not driving a car, it was only the "idea" of what the loss of it implied that was upsetting. This is the perfect example of "identification." And while her well-being did not need to be impaired by its loss, her mind convinced her that it *was* impaired, and so it most definitely was.

In the case of her license and her car, it was the *role* that was coveted, in addition to the *form* comprised of metal, rubber, and glass. Obviously, when these identifications are broken down in this manner, it seems absurd, but that's the point entirely. Such identifications are fleeting and inhibit recognition of your true identification as essence. All strong identifications—each one of them—*is* absurd from a spiritual perspective, given the degree of suffering their inevitable loss creates.

Twelve years prior to my awakening, following my second divorce, I came close to losing all hope for happiness and satisfaction as a result of the loss of my marriage, home, car, and financial standing. During my marriage, I had developed our stunning, five-acre Malibu ranch as a location site for filming, complete with 350 newly planted pepper trees, a gorgeous solar-heated infinity swimming pool, graded helipad, and topped off with my son's beloved horses, pot-bellied pigs, geese, dogs, cats, and his frequently visiting playmates. The life that we created there was an indescribably abundant, fun-loving time with family, financial security, and deeply comfortable and inspiring surroundings. Watching my son and his friends happily bounce on the trampoline against a backdrop of the most stunning view from our mountaintop ranch was indescribably satisfying. And yet, my marriage was crumbling and I couldn't face the inevitable—that soon, every single thing that I cherished would virtually disappear overnight.

This did indeed happen, and to say that I had identified with my surroundings is an understatement. It was inconceivable to me that I would be divested of every single "form" (except my son), including every beloved pet (except two dogs and two pigs). This divesture was complete on all levels, and was torture, plain and simple. My mental suffering produced gallons of tears, depression, and deep grieving for two years, to a degree that I wondered how one woman's eyes could produce so much water.

The cause: identifications with the roles, forms, and attributes that surrounded me. I cherished my role as stay-at-home mother and valued my time with my young son. I loved my role as the wife of a wealthy, intelligent, and kind husband. My forms, the "things" of my daily existence, were near-perfect from the perspective of "largess." There was nothing that was wanting and it was all beautiful, shiny, and comfortable. My attributes were that of a woman who was carefree, happy, comfortable, and spiritually alive.

When those roles, forms, and attributes dissolved, I dissolved, or at least the "little me" that was attached to those identifications. Suddenly, I had no idea who I was, where I was going, the reason for living, or what the reason was for such catastrophic failure—financially, interpersonally, and spiritually.

As a result of this full collapse of my identifications, a deepening occurred, although not the last deepening that would finally bring this lesson all the way home. Looking back now at those identifications and how they were ripped away from me, I realize that losing everything can be very instructive, spiritually speaking. This is not to say that a person must lose everything to grow spiritually. In fact, that's the point of this exercise. We are undertaking the *conscious* process to self-realization. My sudden divestiture of identifications was *not a conscious* process, but rather one imposed upon me by the river of life when my own inner process was not creating this outcome. The goals of the soul are always to grow spiritually. We always have the opportunity to grow consciously, but if we don't, life will take over and help us to go more deeply by ripping away the identifications that bind us. In later years, once recognized as an obstacle to spiritual awareness, my attachments were allowed to bubble up to the surface of my awareness and became entries on my list. This is how it's done, by initially jotting down those areas in which your beloved sense of attachment to roles, forms, and attributes virtually defines who you are. You'll know if you've got one because the very thought of its loss is not even conceivable.

Once each entry has been identified and added to your list, you will consciously undergo a process whereby you, as vividly as possible, imagine that it's gone—vanished, finished from your life—*forever*. Upon beginning this second part of the process, be sure to benefit by accessing the three gateways at the same time. Focus on your breath and the inner energy field of the body, in order to align with your essence while conducting the "exorcism" part of the exercise. Take several long, deep breaths, in and out, and allow the breath to take you inside. Remember, you aren't doing anything; it's your *essence* that is the active principle in play here, so just surrender to the process and allow it to do its job.

This process, although perhaps *initially* upsetting or uncomfortable, will bring to life what freedom really is: freedom from false identities. It is extremely liberating to be free from the identification with false roles; freedom from identification with false forms and freedom from identification with false attributes.

The purpose of this practice is to artificially demonstrate to you what the process of enlightenment feels like, what those sparkling new eyes will perceive. In other words, once you have attained self-realization, what is gone are the embedded, strong dysfunctional ties to roles, forms, and attributes that you formerly would have fought hard to keep, and had you lost them, suffering would have ensued. I'm not suggesting that, in order to awaken, you must give up all relationships and all your stuff and become a wandering ascetic; however, conscious awakening requires that you attain some degree of dis-identification from chronic roles, forms, and attributes that masquerade as *you*. The very definition of "self-realization" is when you know for certain the nature of your true self. Freedom, spiritual freedom, is the only true success. No amount of worldly accomplishment or gain can promise chronic peace and well-being. The only real success is a successful present moment, wherein you finally know the truth of who you are, and live that truth as a waking principle in your life. As such, it is necessary for you to now actually taste the nectar of this freedom, wherein all the losses that you have been defending against, whether consciously or unconsciously, are finally out in the open and you can look at them squarely in the light of day. As you delve deeper into this practice, notice the suffering attached to your belief that you *need and want* these roles, forms, and attributes for happiness, or even for survival.

As this practice is described, you may notice that your mind is objecting. This is to be expected, of course, as in any effective spiritual practice, the mind won't like it. In this case particularly, because so many seekers have been schooled in the practice of visualization and manifestation in order to get more goodies in life, this practice may sound just plain *wrong*. You may be objecting, countering that you've spent hundreds of hours attempting to precisely imagine the *gaining* of desired roles, forms, or attributes. Indeed, you may have been working very diligently to increase their numbers, to add, not subtract, them from your life.

To the surprise of the ego, the power of this practice comes from actually imagining your life as though each item were already absent with no hope whatsoever of the possibility of regaining or replacing it. Although I use the word imagine, the power of the process cannot really be accessed by simple imagination, but by viscerally pretending through an ever-deepening use of imagination, that you have just come face-to-face with the knowledge that this (item on your list) is now gone forever, with no possible hope of it ever returning.

It's impossible to present this exercise without addressing your mind's probable objection that (gasp) isn't it *bad* to focus on an outcome that you don't want? Self-help and abundance-creation guidebooks all point to the power of intention, and how you can use the power of the mind to create an outcome or get lots of goodies, by visualizing its presence already obtained or achieved. In other words, if you want a red Ferrari, just visualize it sitting in your driveway; if you want a lover, simply fluff up the pillow next to you; if you want to win the marathon, visualize breaking the tape at the course's end and feel your aching, but triumphant legs splayed on the massage table.

This "abundance creation model," although enabling accumulation and achievement, presupposes that more future is needed in order to feel happy or satisfied. Its use cancels out entirely the truth that you need nothing more than this moment in order to feel peace and be endowed with a permanent sense of well-being, *right now*. Further, the visualization model, at its core, uses the concept of imagining an outcome, which is a thought, which is matter. As we've already discussed, your highest, most effective and creative abilities are borne from a source which is the *opposite* of matter. So when you focus on matter as the route to achieving a goal, you are focusing on a lesser god, so to speak. Instead, by focusing on "nothing"—"no-thing"—the deepest essence of you, you align with a power that is *more* potent, stillness. Then, once this alignment is in place, the river of life will handle all your true needs in the most extraordinarily magical way possible.

You may have erroneously believed that you needed to bait a hook and go fishing for the goodies in life; but now you know differently. Simply take your fishing pole and throw it in the shed. Instead, place *yourself* in the river of life and let go of the bank. Whatever fish are necessary to enhance the blueprint of your life, as defined by your soul, will swim upstream against all odds like a salmon in order to reach you. This doesn't mean that you don't take any action or respond to any fish that are swimming in your direction. It means that the river of life can be entrusted to support you. It, more than your egoic thought structure, knows your deepest needs, which are actually very few and have to do with your soul's purpose. Only the river of life knows the timing and details of how to best wash you ashore at the right destination. Hence, the "chasing" paradigm, in which you accumulate stuff by visualizing it, or capture unsuspecting romantic partners by visualizing them—is a dead end. Sorry to burst your egoic bubble, but those things and people who will truly enhance your life, as determined by the river of life, may be so "foreign" that you probably have no *clue* as to what they really are anyway. So how can you properly manifest it through visualization? Your soul plan, as held by the essence of you, knows what is needed. Your pain body knows some things too, but only in the world of gnashing teeth and misery. So which result sounds better?

That's why this exercise, in which you let go of previously held beliefs about what is important, is so *powerful*. For the first time in a long time, you are going to drop all your preconceived ideas as to what *should* be attained and what should be let go. Then, you finally become truly open to receiving that which you really do need for your soul's blueprint. Such a blueprint has to do with how you are here to contribute to the healing of the world, which ultimately is only effective as you heal yourself through awakening, spiritually.

In my own case, my blueprint was to drop a six-figure salaried position to become a caregiver for an Alzheimer's patient, having no previous experience in this field. This leap into the unknown was spurred on by my recognizing that my strong identification to recent roles as author and officer manager was holding me back. There was a point, just prior to my acceptance of my position as caregiver, that I gave up the pursuit of goals because I suddenly recognized that I actually had no idea what course or direction was really good for me. From that void came this position. It was out of this surrendering to "not know" that a more vital knowing ultimately developed. My inner blueprint was unknown to me until it presented itself.

Because you have been so mind-dominated up to this point, what makes you think that you know what your blueprint is? If you recall, in the previous chapters we have been discussing all the ways that the mind causes you trouble and blocks your true nature as a contented being. Now you have an opportunity through applying this exercise with courage and focus, to actually wipe clean your list of assumptions and allow the river of life to carry you to your appropriate shore. Whatever goodies and people and enhancements will add to your particular new, more conscious life, will practically be hurled in your direction with no need for angst or compulsive planning.

This does not suggest that you will cease all action; to the contrary, whatever action you implement will now be managing what the river of life delivers to your doorstep. Gone are the days where you take your canoe and paddle hard upstream against the current to get things. Now, you are aligning more fully with presence and as such, you are aligning more fully with your own— perhaps still unknown, yet ever present—soul's plan.

The inherent effectiveness of the power of intention and visualization is real; however, instead of using this principle to obtain a new car, start a new career path, upgrade to a better house, or to find a mate, use your intention to align with your essence. From that standpoint, once self-realization is uncovering itself, all other "things" and "destinations," both career and personal, will be revealed as a natural outpouring of fully existing in the river of life. What is needed will come to you. *It* will chase *you.* If it's not really needed for your now *higher purpose,* then the river of life won't wash you ashore where it exists. You don't need to chase after unsuitable spouses or lose sleep in competing for a better job. Visualize, if you must, the flowering of your own consciousness. Enlightenment truly is the only goal that, if achieved, produces guaranteed, lasting results that align with the goals of your soul. Only from that stance will you actually know and then visualize what is really needed and wanted by your essence. Otherwise, the imbecile that is doing the visualization is your pain body. Do you really want *it* as the architect of your life?

When we speak about manifesting desired outcomes or

things, there comes a point when all spiritual practitioners must come to terms with precisely what is the most important aspect of their life. What is it that you *truly* desire? If you desire self-realization above all else, then your true self must be realized. This sounds simple enough, but are you aware that almost every single ingrained, strong, cultural identification counteracts this realization? That's the whole point of the challenge in attaining while remaining *in* the culture. That's why it has been so rare, up until now, for anyone to awaken, let alone a seeker who defies the usual route of asceticism. Because so many of us have accumulated a lot of nice things, traveled the world, fallen in love—but still, that inner call to awaken loudly chimes—we are beginning to suspect that something is amiss with the cultural definition of what real "success" is. No matter what we earn, win, attain, or achieve, there's still something missing. What's missing is the ultimate freedom, in knowing the truth of who you are, and the resulting peace that this realization brings. This is when accumulating for its own sake and upholding false images are recognized as a trap to the awakening process.

One of the most common questions about attaining self-realization is, must a seeker stop all work projects, give up all goals, leave the family and kids, and donate everything to charity? The answer is "no," but with one very important caveat: The desire for self-realization must be held as primary above all else, and you must begin to uncover the recognition that *you* are complete, *without* any of these roles, forms, and attributes. In addition, even the goal of achieving enlightenment eventually must be surrendered, to allow the perfection of the present moment to be appreciated, without need of anything more.

The recognition that you are truly complete without anything else needing to be added, cannot simply be another theoretical concept or one more idea that you add to your other ideas.

It must be a very real, working recognition that, once truly *experienced*, brings immense *relief*. Initially the prospect of losing all the entries on your list brings profound panic, fear, and grief, but now you know without a shadow of a doubt that, although you might enjoy and appreciate them, they are not necessary for your peace and well-being. Again, this cannot be a mere intellectual understanding. It must be a deep-feeling recognition from your innermost being, wherein you know your completeness requires nothing outside of yourself.

Because self-realization is a *permanent* state of well-being and is not tied to the transiency of roles, forms, or attributes, you will discover that true inner peace awaits you right now. Once experienced, you discover that it can always be experienced. No longer must you be confused that something or someone is needed for your ability to be at peace. That's why enlightenment is the only true freedom. As the normal process of life brings with it untold and potentially alarming changes and loss from the mind's perspective, your new and appropriate identification with *self*, envelops you in peace despite any outward chaos.

The self-realized person can still happily own property, maintain thriving monogamous relationships and be married, maintain health insurance and establish a college fund for the kids; however, they are secondary to the one true alignment with your essence. All can be added, but once added and then lost, it does not really matter that much. Of course, sadness is still experienced when a loved one leaves this world, and when you behold the pain and suffering of those *in* the world. But you will never, ever lose yourself again as those losses occur. There's no depression, or long-standing grief, and most certainly, there is no "story" that you tell yourself and others, regarding your loss with all its attendant drama and attention-getting ploys.

## Identify Cherished "Roles"

So let's get started. In the first column under "Roles," hone in on identifications to roles that you consider to be super important for your happiness. Once you complete your entries in this category, then fill in the two additional columns: one of "Forms" (things) and the other column for your "Attributes."

Of course, everyone's list will vary according to their ingrained preferences and perceptions.

Many people, particularly older people, are deeply attached to their role as sufferer of a physical malady or injury. They may talk about their pain and suffering, and although they do not often notice it, they become deeply attached to their story about their own suffering. In many instances, we may witness others who cry or moan about rather insignificant events, and we have struggled with how exactly it is that we should appropriately respond.

When we support another's dysfunctional role by acknowledging their emotional pain with such comments as, "I understand that you're upset," rather than acknowledging their inner being, it actually bolsters the pain body. Of course, the pain body is upset. It exists for only this reason and so it relishes our concession that it's upset or angry, because it deeply yearns for us to notice its suffering. By "acknowledging" another's pain, we presume that this strategy will reduce their suffering, yet this is almost never the case. When you "enable" any sufferer or DP's role-playing in this manner, it only *ensures* the continuation of the nightmare that their plight is indeed catastrophic. Rather than acknowledge another's pain as a result of a habitual role, instead gently wake the person up from the nightmare by reminding them of the tender gift of life. Rather than collude with the nightmare of self-pity that runs rampant through most every ego-based pain body, instead be a giver of life and help uncover the real truth: no amount of drama or negative response will change what *is*. And what *is* has no inherent problem within it. When reduced down to simply *this moment,* all is well. There may be actions that are necessary, but those actions can only be addressed in the perfection of the present moment. Rather than agreeing that trivial negative reactions are in any way justified, help your children, your DP—or yourself—to see through enlightened eyes, wherein suffering is self-created by our roles and unnecessary.

*If you really, truly want to help someone, help them to see the perfection of what is. But do not conspire with them by attempting to communicate that you, too, out of so-called "compassion," are willing to see the "catastrophe" through their eyes. Instead, be the awakener of dreamers: Help awaken them from the illusion of self-pity.*

This human tendency to align with a victim's role and to keep telling stories about current and past hurts, perhaps is the reason why so many people are willing to continue under the tutelage of spiritual teachers or therapists for years without any appreciable gains. The teacher unwittingly acknowledges the reality of the "nightmare," thereby creating a feeding frenzy of self-pity and self-importance for the pain body. Most people react similarly to changes or delays with equal emotional force, even when their lives are blessed by extraordinary privileges unknown by most of the world.

When you consider the plight of the majority of humans on the planet, it's incredible how thoroughly the mind has a person spewing tapes of self-pity. If ever there is a common role played by most everyone, it's that of the victim. A gauge of the degree of your spiritual maturity is if chronic storytelling about problems occurs frequently. So in the preparation of your list with respect to roles, don't forget to consider your role as victim and how you rerun that tape to your parents, partner, therapist, or friends.

Now, let's get back to the list identifying your cherished roles. Do you strongly identify with a sport or activity that includes physical agility? Then, if for some reason the sport cannot be performed, suffering will occur. It is common to seek outdoor activities as a means of relaxation; however, suppose you are unable to partake of the sport? What happens to your sense of well-being? When you make inner peace and serenity conditional upon certain activities, you limit your ability to remain becalmed when it's not available or you're unable to perform.

For example, you may consider that you're a good golfer, and you identify "golfer" as one of your roles. You may play golf frequently, or you may shop for golf paraphernalia; your closest friends may be golfers, or you often watch golf tournaments on television. No matter your handicap, you readily relate to the world of golf. It's one of your roles. It's a preferred activity that helps you relax or unwind from a busy week. Your social calendar frequently includes trips to the golf course. You try to schedule golf practice or golf games as much as possible. So add golfer to your list, under the "roles" heading.

When you have identified golfer as one of your cherished roles, now begin part two of the process. Imagine that you can no longer play the sport at all. Picture your weekend arriving, and not driving to the golf course. Where will you now go for peace? Instead of allowing the mind to identify a replacement "role," such as to take up sailing, the purpose of the exercise is to surrender to its absence, and to find the underlying peace that is already there, despite the fact that there is no golf to bring it to you.

When golf is your sole and preferred method of relaxation, what happens to your ability to relax if you get a bad back or your knee goes out? This is the purpose of the exercise: to make you aware of how your peace is contingent on your alignment with something else—whether a role, form, or attribute.

What other roles are important to you? You may include your profession, or you may not feel any particular identification with your job or line of work. That's fine; however, most people have a very real, deeply ingrained identification with their profession. If you cannot imagine being separated from your profession without any emotional or physical discomfort of any kind, then add it to your list. For example, if you are a doctor, imagine for a moment that suddenly your license to practice medicine is revoked, and you must find another way to make a living. In doing this exercise, avoid all mental reservations that this outcome would probably never happen. Never mind that in "real life," you would hire an attorney to fight to get it back, or that all your friends and family know that it is just a temporary glitch. Forget all that. This exercise requires that you add any role that if, for whatever reason, it were to be really, truly gone from your life, it would upset you; this it is a candidate for your list.

Once identified, now begin the process of letting it go. Suddenly, you are no longer aligned with the role of doctor. Where will you now get your sense of identity, importance, and self-respect? Allow yourself to fully imagine that you can no longer use this professional role as an identification; who are you underneath that role?

Next, consider other roles, such as that of parent, grandparent, spouse, lover, mother, father, sibling, daughter, son, employee, employer, dog owner, horseback rider, spiritual seeker, or yogi, etc. Imagine that whatever makes this role possible suddenly vanishes. For example, are you a mother of a small child? If you are, it is highly likely that your role of mother has probably usurped all other roles, even to your own or others' detriment. Before you object that this is the natural way of things, just add mother to the list. If even considering the disappearance of any of your roles would cause you anguish, then add it to the list.

As you proceed with your list, notice how your mind objects. It won't want you to add your role as parent or grandparent. We are so highly superstitious that many believe that merely doing this exercise, in and of itself, will potentially jeopardize your role. Isn't that interesting? We are afraid of visualizing an outcome that we say that we don't want; however, you are most likely unaware of the intensity and repetition of your compulsive thinking to forestall this very outcome. In other words, your sensitivity is proof positive that you're already spending untold repetitive thoughts worrying about the role's stability and ensuring that "it" never leaves you.

Sometimes it's our neurotic preoccupations and behaviors that point to the degree of identification with one of our roles. For example, any parent who has been accused of being a control freak, or is intentionally focused on the minutia relating to their charge, is actually exhibiting deep fear and insecurity regarding the potential loss of their coveted role. As such, an entry belongs on the list if it causes upset when you imagine the absence of the other who makes your role possible, like a child. If that prospect has you breaking into a sweat or if it produces a gentle panic or if you feel annoyed at the very suggestion of this exercise, add that entry to your list. If you've broken out in hives or if you're already in tears, congratulations, you're correctly identifying the roles that belong on your list.

In the event that you recognize a role as being very coveted, you can guarantee that you are unwittingly causing suffering for others in your immediate environment. Where there is dysfunctional identification with a role, form, or attribute, there is fear of the loss of it. Where there is fear, there is always neurosis. If you doubt that this is the case, just ask someone who lives or works with you if they secretly believe that you have become somewhat neurotic within the context of this role. Although you may think no one else notices the degree of your neurosis, they do and have been affected by it. Of course, you have to muster the courage to really ask others to be honest with you for your own good. Chances are, you have been holding your entire household or work environment hostage by your actions as a control freak, based on your rigid identification with a role, form, or attribute.

Suppose that you realize that you are overly identified with your role as parent. Perhaps you suspect that you have a "hurried child" or that you derive vicarious satisfaction from the child's accomplishments, and thus you push the child as a means to bolster your own identity. Another aspect of a strong identification with this role is to be neurotically focused on the minutia of your child's every function and reaction. This is quite common, of course, and is considered to be "normal" parenting. Be that as it may, it's still dysfunctional and, unchecked, causes suffering for both parent and child.

You may be wondering, once the role of parent is added to the list, just how does a parent go about "disappearing" their role—in their imagination—to fully participate in this spiritual practice? Remember, this practice is designed to reduce suffering by being aware of how your roles, forms, and attributes block recognition of your true essence. It's possible that you are not yet ready to actually implement this exercise as a working process in attaining self-realization. This is fine, and as was already stated, not every spiritual student is "ripe" nor is everyone's timing the same when it comes to uncovering your true, unchanging nature. However, by just having read about this spiritual practice, even without putting it into practice, you have still become more informed as to right-alignment with respect to roles, forms, and attributes. Given the suffering caused by too rigidly identifying with one of your roles, there may come a time in the future when this practice can be implemented for the benefit of all.

Using this same example with respect to your role as parent, it is helpful to begin where you first dissolve the identification with that of you, as a person. What I mean to say is, first you must imagine that you—meaning your physical body—are no longer alive, due to fire, flood, death, illness, etc. This means that you will first visualize—in the quiet of your room or while alone at the beach—your own death. It is not necessary to imagine the *cause* of death. You are simply to imagine, with closed eyes if necessary, that you have died. The most effective route to this end is to simply imagine and visualize your own rotting corpse.

This may seem extreme or it may seem unnecessary, but it is a *vital* step in dissolving an identification with anything. That's why you may as well start with the hardest "role" on the list. So do it now: simply imagine your own body, at the age you are right now, in the active stage of a decomposing, rotting corpse. Don't forget to access the three gateways while being immersed in this meditation. Focus on your breath and the inner energy field of the body to more fully align with the deepest part of yourself. Whenever you consciously use breath focus within a context of upset or difficulty, make a point to breathe in slowly and deeply, at least several times, which will immediately slow down compulsive thought.

There you are, minus your stylish clothes, your "appendages": such as your jewelry, car, big house, suntan, health-club membership, and all your other means for happiness. Imagine the finality of your body, now finished. Your teeth are not brushed. Needless to say, you look terrible. Your body is indeed at its absolute worst, because it's dead and decomposing. (Are you still focused on your breath and the inner energy field of the body while you visualize this?)

So, there you are, rotting. Imagine how silly and unhelpful all those roles, forms, and attributes are at this juncture. All the physical exercise and nutrition regimens did not forestall it. Of course, you have justified all the stuff and effort throughout your life as a means to ensure the *quality* of life while you were living. Of course, such enhancements do make a difference in your life; however, this does not mean that you are immune from the way of all form, which is dissolution. We all know of people who, despite their wealth and health, still succumb to serious illnesses or injuries. When this happens, many of them lose the desire to live, even when their lives are far from over. This is an identification with the way the body used to be and one's health as it once was. An inability to stay in the present moment, as forms and conditions change, causes extreme suffering.

For the student of spirituality, the changing nature of form must be addressed if self-realization—identification with your true essence—is to be uncovered. If you want to be free, you must be willing to know the nature of what binds you. We've already discussed identifications with mental thought, and now we must uncover identifications with roles, forms, and attributes.

To be able to objectively observe the reality of your own rotting corpse is profoundly freeing. (In fact, meditating at cremation grounds is a spiritual practice in India.) Allow your imagination to fully sink into this realization. Imagine how all your cherished loved ones will be entrusted to their own lives, without you hovering nearby and managing their happiness and safety. This specific practice, wherein you come to terms with the fact that you and your most cherished loves ones will not escape death, is remarkably freeing. When you actually "see" this reality in a living, breathing, yet deeply personal meditation, a crack in the egoic shell occurs. Of course, there is initial discomfort, but then the reality of your plight, and that of us all, is surrendered to. What relief! What profound joy to know, finally, that there is more to *you* than the play of form. *Underneath* the form is *you*, an unchanging purity of essence that is forever part of the aqua blue sea and the azure sky that goes on forever.

Once you have survived the recognition of your own death; then add those people you love the most, allowing their bodies to be what they already *are:* changeable, impermanent, and subject to the natural rhythm of all life forms. This will free you from a preoccupation with the lie that, by intently micromanaging their well-being, their eventual outcome will somehow escape its normal course. When we can let go of those whom we most love, they are forever a part of us now. Finally, their true relationship to us is revealed: they are identical to our own essence; they too are aligned with the source of all life, and in fact, they too *are* life, so how can they ever truly disappear?

Next, after you have identified all the obvious roles, such as parent or spouse, etc., identify all the roles with which you have become so aligned that they have taken you over. If you cannot imagine yourself without that role, then add it to your list. Ingrained roles permeate the very way that you think of yourself. Actions and habits from these roles constitute your daily life and how you spend your free time, your professional workweek, or even the time that you spend with your family. Roles define the way that you act; they identify your purchasing habits, traveling preferences, and identify your general way of life. Your cherished roles indicate the people in whom you've placed a great deal of importance. But when those people change or leave, suffering occurs.

Naturally, our most cherished roles will usually be made up of interpersonal relationships with loved ones. Yet by definition, each loved one is packaged in a body that is unstable and temporary. We may not be able to tolerate that simple fact, but this is the way of life. Bodies are temporary. When we place our entire identity and source of fulfillment in something that is inherently vulnerable to change and dissolution, suffering is guaranteed.

Many of our most cherished roles have to do with our ability to earn a living and support our families. Imagine how much suffering can occur if you lose your job and are then unable to properly support your family. Not only is the role of breadwinner lost, but the role of "financially responsible role model" is also gone as it relates to your spouse and children. You can see how loaded our ingrained roles have become, and as those roles change and dissolve and then new roles emerge and expand, our egoic thought structure balks. Then mental suffering occurs.

For example, in my own case, I had actually started my list several years prior to awakening and explored my then coveted role as sales director at the publishing company which also published my books. When I left the company, I left one role as a sales director, but also my role as author needed to be explored as a cherished identity that needed excising. Although I continued to book a few more radio interviews, there was a very strong pull to let go of the role of author. As such, I began to seek employment outside of the field of publishing. Indeed, there was a temporary period during which I was unemployed altogether, and that status caused resistance and stress, even though it was I who had initiated the change.

Although I was soon hired as an office manager by the surgical practice in Beverly Hills, I left that position after two years, despite the fact that I was earning a very good salary. As I began to initiate this specific spiritual practice, I recognized that I had developed a very real identification with *many* different roles and that, as they dissolved or changed, I suffered greatly. When I left the surgical practice, I grieved the loss of income, and I felt a warm panic arising within me. Through reflection, I recognized that the suffering I was experiencing was due to a strong identification with my income because I told myself that I had earned it through reputation and hard work. To me, it was a source of pride. It wasn't just the income that I enjoyed but the knowledge that I, as a woman and as a one-time single mother, had broken through all the obstacles blocking professional success and had created a "role" for myself in spite of the challenges. This was also the case with that of my role as an author.

Through painful reflection, I recognized an egoic need to play this role. It was amazing to finally so clearly recognize a strong egoic need to uphold a particular self-image and to conceive of myself as an author and speaker. As such, after deep reflection, I felt that I was left with a very painful choice: relinquish my author role or cease to awaken spiritually. After fully embracing this decision, I was amazed at how freeing the process actually was. What a relief! Suddenly, there was no need to be anything at all. The dreaded deed had finally been done, and I ceased seeking my most coveted role as a means to find satisfaction and well-being.

Of course, in your own case, it may not be viable for you to actually dissolve *your* coveted role in a literal way; however, by deeply meditating upon the dissolution of your own favorite roles, a similar recognition can still be experienced, and the role can again be taken up but with more detachment. Further, once this practice is conducted, if that role should actually dissolve at some time in the future, imagine how prepared you will be, spiritually speaking.

In my own case, even after I quit my role as author, my books were still in print and the publisher still mailed me periodic royalty statements; however, I decided that no new books or projects would be forthcoming. At one point, I even phoned my publisher, asking him to place my books out of print, which he refused to do. But no matter, in my deepest understanding, my strong identification with the author role had been totally dissolved.

Now free from this coveted role, an enormous well of peace began to emerge. Soon, I recognized that serenity was available now, no matter what I was doing. This was a huge turning point for me: to really, truly, with no holdbacks, unequivocally dissolve my most cherished role, with others soon to follow. The freedom and relief was palpable. While meditating upon this dis-identification, I found inside who I truly am, and that realization of self produced a profound spiritual deepening. It was then that the river of life was able to flow me straight to Jeannette's door to take up the unexpected position as her caregiver. But even as I took up this new role, I could still participate in the workaday world of earning a salary and paying the bills, and it no longer mattered what vehicle produced this. Any action became suddenly satisfying.

Ironically, like peeling back the layers of an onion, the next role that I recognized as a cherished identity was that of the role of "spiritual seeker." Then, that role, too, had to be relinquished, and I contemplated the very real possibility that I would never experience enlightenment, no matter what I did or how much I improved, or how much "time" had elapsed, including future lifetimes.

At first, this possibility was alarming, inasmuch as it was of great interest to me, and was the reason behind all my extraterrestrial contact experiences and included all my clairvoyant and clairaudient inspirations. For decades, I had been awakened out of my sleep to witness extraordinary visions and audible messages that inspired me to participate more fully in the process of my own spiritual awakening. As a result, like many spiritual seekers, enlightenment became one of my most cherished desires and goals. And yet, I could not ignore the recognition that the egoic thought structure was even successful in co-opting *this* goal and my role as spiritual seeker. This recognition was horrifying to me. If the ego had found an inroad into the very goal of spiritual attainment, then no goal was chaste, nor could I automatically assume that any offer of help was genuine without egoic enhancement.

This recognition that the ego would naturally co-opt every possible goal for its own embellishment produced a new deepening of my perspective. If enlightenment were even possible, then it could only be attained in the humble context of agreeing to be "used" by my essence as a helper, no matter the way or form requested. In other words, *if* it were possible to awaken, then I became willing to use that new alignment with presence in the most basic, low-profile way imaginable. I even pictured myself as having attained enlightenment and joyously working at McDonald's or cleaning houses. This meant that my new purpose after enlightenment would be solely to hold a space of peace for others or of service, and no type of work or environment was too limiting, too simple, or too distasteful to qualify. My agreement with essence/life became restated: if there was any chance whatsoever that awakening was possible for me, then I humbly agreed to carry out ordinary work in an ordinary environment while remaining free of reactivity, and thus being a bringer of peace. This became my new understanding of how my potential awakening would unfold.

But this new, refined "role" was not possible until my former roles, as co-opted by the ego, had been completely exorcised. This became an in-depth spiritual exorcism in its own right. When it was clearly understood that there was no equivocation possible if I had any hope of awakening, then it actually became a possibility for me. There could be no thread remaining regarding a secret desire for ego enhancement. Then, and only then, could my "New Deal" be born into existence.

Once I properly understood the task at hand, in now brutally identifying all those areas (roles, forms, and attributes) that held false ego enhancement attached to them, would I be able to awaken spiritually. This new possibility to awaken necessarily required an agreement that I would dedicate my life to the benefit of others who shared this objective, without concern for the mechanics of how that process would unfold.

Despite my own personal search for an enlightened state, this is hardly a goal that everyone shares, but many do indeed wish to live in a state of chronic well-being. Case in point is Jeannette's own husband. By simply recognizing the mechanics of the pain body and by observing his own mental processes, he has himself dramatically improved his own sense of peace and well-being and yet he is still very effective professionally. He now shares his insights regularly with co-workers and friends, and even has achieved a more sustained peaceful context for his trial work with opposing counsel. He reports that this new context has ironically produced more effectiveness within a business setting, not less.

There is a silent power derived from an alignment with presence that is not available to those who attempt to demonstrate authority by using confrontational aggressiveness. This new, silent power is accessed and activated when you align with presence—instead of using aggressive confrontation—and is of an altogether different order of effectiveness within a business environment. Although it may initially seem counter-intuitive to adopt a calm demeanor and alignment with presence's power—when one would normally attempt to dominate or control an outcome using aggression—actually, aligning with presence is always life enhancing and is ultimately the only guarantee that the right and correct response and action will be undertaken for the benefit of all. The more competitive and combative a business environment, the more crucial it is to align with presence and to access the three gateways by focusing on the breath and placing your attention on the inner energy field of the body. This, then, is the new paradigm for use within a context of a competitive and combative business environment and is the only guarantee that right action becomes aligned with right timing. When the mind is quiet, the most appropriately inspired words and actions are able to move through you and to then be expressed by you. As such, they are expressed more judiciously and effectively than words and actions that are derived from mental activity alone.

Jeannette's husband described how once, during a heated legal mediation meeting with opposing counsel who was verbally antagonistic, he suddenly recognized the negative dynamics in play. He then told them and the judge that he had no interest in engaging in an angry verbal duel, and that as a seeker of his own well-being chose to go forward with their discussion without angry or defensive reactions. This produced a surprising yet beneficial outcome for all. Several mouths dropped open, and even the attorneys on his team stared at him in disbelief. Later one of them said that he could hardly believe that he, of all people, could shrug off an opposing counsel's verbal attack without a negative response, saying, "Either you were drinking at lunch or you fell on your head."

Considered to be an aggressive trial lawyer, with a winner-take-all style, he has hugely benefitted from simple but effective spiritual practice. Ironically, even when adding more presence within the context of competitive trial work, he reports that he is still effective and has not turned to mush. It has made quite a difference to him in the quality of his professional life, and with respect to his inner process as his own wife moves closer to passing on.

As such, the benefits of softening identifications with roles, forms, and attributes do not only benefit the formal spiritual practitioner. Anyone at all who simply yearns for more peace in their lives, free of drama and chronic moodiness, can easily readily benefit. Naturally, as more peace arises within you, everything else begins to function more effectively. That is the gift of presence.

As I relinquished the need to control the aspects as to *how* the process would unfold as I surrendered my strong identification with the role of spiritual seeker, a deeper peace was achieved. Such statement does not mean that I relinquished my ability to support myself or to earn a living in the context of modern life. Once I had relinquished all goals and identities around being an author, or the goal of earning a lot of money, then, post-enlightenment, a new book arose within me—but the success or notoriety of that new book were not at all my concern or focus. As creative expression flowed through me, the new book easily completed itself in exactly eight weeks while I was working fulltime and with Jeannette in the final stage of Alzheimer's. However, there was the palpable recognition that the new work was not mine, nor was it of *me;* rather, it belonged to life. As such, there was no more "role" associated with it. There I was at my laptop writing, in between tubal feedings and doing the laundry, but there was no identity associated with "author" or the hope that it would rescue me from the "perfection" of washing dishes or doing laundry. So-called professional success, even when it occurs, like everything else, is fleeting and subject to change and dissolution. As such, no satisfaction can ever be found from identifying with the role that produced the success.

During the process of effective spiritual practice leading to the actual enlightenment experience, the ego's roots need to be excised. They run deeply through all of us, and once this recognition occurs without embarrassment and is implemented with courage and insight, a new being is born. It goes without saying that this realization happens in the present moment. Although spiritual practice is initiated and is continued over time, this does not mean that more "time" is needed for awakening. You, as pure essence, is all you need right now. This recognition is, therefore, possible at this very moment. No future is needed for right understanding and self-recognition—"self-realization."

As we have discussed, the ego exists to blow itself up with importance so that its safety feels guaranteed. It's desperately afraid of the future. This is its function and one that, on an evolutionary scale, has been inherently expanding as part of human mental development since *Homo sapiens* first wielded clubs. Now, for the first time in human evolution, spiritual development is taking precedence over mental dominance, which will result in a quiet mind and thus the uncovering of presence. As a result, human relationships and all of humanity benefit tremendously from a lessened egoic stance. And in case you're wondering what effect this process has on IQ levels, it actually increases because your *entire* essence is uncovered, leaving more of *you* available for right action and creativity. Creative, productive, and true and lasting solutions to "problems"—in addition to right livelihood being the focus without stress and harm to others—can finally be identified and implemented for the benefit of all. The way and manner of the egoic mind structure, with its dysfunctional pattern of negative reaction, is on the way out as a "fashionably normal" set of behaviors. The strong focus on tomorrow is dying out as humanity's standard operating procedure, which produced no end to suffering.

Enlightenment means that you have successfully navigated through the vehement objections of the ego, mind, and pain body and have triumphantly uncovered your full presence in this moment of now. However, the journey to enlightenment is not really a journey at all because awakening can only happen in the same way that *any* experience happens, which is in the present moment. Although this seems like semantics, it is actually a very real alignment in perception that shifts your focus to the now, away from future tripping and past remorse.

Future tripping is what you commonly do when you place your hopes and dreams for happiness and satisfaction in the future. What is hardly noticed is that when an arbitrary future date arrives, it is always experienced in the present moment. Has it brought happiness and satisfaction with it? Or is more future needed to again forestall satisfaction away from right now. When you focus on some future project or objective, you can still do so without getting stuck there. This type of planning uses "clock time"—as Tolle refers to it—as a necessary function of life; however, once the focus on future events or plans has been completed, you put the mind back down, returning your focus to the present moment.

In the same way that you would put down a hammer after you use this tool for a project, you also place the mind back down when you're finished with it. You do not allow the hammer to start hitting you on the head, which is the way most people's minds run them around, objecting to this or to that, and identifying with all sorts of roles, forms, and attributes that, when changed or lost, create intense suffering.

Naturally, once enlightened, you will continue to take on roles, but they will be very temporary as you complete one task after another. In the same way that a chef removes his hat at the end of the day; so, too, will you "put down" your role as a temporary identity the moment you complete a project that requires it. The chef, when he goes home to his children, is no longer a chef, but instead a father and husband. In the same manner, the enlightened person may take up a role, but it will be like a character in a play, very short-lived and not a real identity. At this moment, I am writing a manuscript, which creates the role of author. But from my new perspective, this temporary role will only be taken up again when I sit down to write for an hour or two. When I'm finished writing, my "author role" ends. In the meantime, it has no further import than does the role of bather as I take a shower.

When you *consciously* use clock time as a means to focus on some creative project, plan a vacation, create a last will and testament, or schedule a dentist appointment, you are using time appropriately. Heretofore, your thoughts were virtually focused on nothing *other* than the future or the past. Now, you are aware of your mind as you use it to think about plans and projects, but you then cease thinking about them and return to a quiet mind in the present moment. *Can you see the qualitative difference between these two states of being?*

Because so many spiritual seekers have been on the path for many years—decades in many cases—it can become a habit to conceive of attaining the wonder of enlightenment after more "time" has elapsed. Seekers themselves, as I did, get stuck in future tripping with respect to their own goals of enlightenment. In addition, they come to believe that something else must happen first before a burst of self-realization can occur.

Although it's accurate to say that even this spiritual practice with respect to identifying identifications takes place over a certain amount of time, the problem becomes that even when more time is added, the mind is still searching for resolution and satisfaction in the future. Since the mind exists with a compulsive tendency to avoid the now at all costs, it can't do anything *other* than *delay* its stamp of approval for the experience of satisfaction.

The spiritual seeker who is "ripening" knows a spiritual practice can only be effective when practiced in the present moment. An entirely new way of looking at the world is required in which, at least some of the time, the eyes are looking and experiencing while the mind is silent. The constant need for labeling what is seen dissolves. By using effective spiritual practice such as this one, at least half of your waking hours are experienced with a quiet mind beholding the true nature of *you*. Then, as you ripen further, the mind is quieter than it is noisy.

Although the term spiritual "seeker" is commonly used to identify a person who is seeking enlightenment, they must reorient to the idea that attainment would make them a "finder." In the same way some university students, who identify with their role as student, have trouble graduating and moving beyond a school environment into professional life, the seeker also benefits from forestalling enlightenment and transitioning to actually living an enlightened life right now. As such, consider right now that you are no longer a "seeker" but a "finder"—putting into place the right context for awakening. From this point forward in this text, the term spiritual seeker will be replaced with that of "finder."

Even though we agree that effective spiritual practice occurs over "time," we still behold the present moment right now, just as it is. So act in a way, right now, that demonstrates your enlightenment. Conduct a thorough investigation of all your cherished roles, forms, and attributes as though you are looking out through enlightened eyes right now. "Be" an enlightened one right now, becoming aware of how egoic motivation trickles through your every action. Notice your words and deeds, and most especially, your refusal to agree with the mind's insistence that problems and difficult people lurk everywhere. When you finally catch your mind feeling superior when telling stories of your troubles or pointing out problems or problematic people, you'll know that presence is arising within you. Be the objective observer of your mind as it tries to tell its stories of suffering. With this objectivity the dis-identification process has begun. When you begin to suspect, that simply by virtue of your mind having a thought doesn't mean that the thought is *true*, you are aligning more fully with peace.

In my case, as a *simple* and low-profile desire to just be of service arose within me, enlightenment became possible. When you're ready to be of service, the river of life meanders back to your doorstep to help you do just that; however, the intention must be pure. You cannot trick the universe. The egoic habit of co-opting spiritual gains must be recognized as a predictable response as you awaken through spiritual practice. Unless this is dissolved, however, enlightenment is not attained; or rather, you may flip-flop back and forth, creating stress again with egoic demands.

*True spiritual attainment is the ability to experience the profundity of the present moment. A desire to be of service in the moment is the only appropriate inspiration when approaching or completing a goal that is said to serve this end.*

Recently, I was sitting at the table writing when the doorbell rang. Opening the door, I found a young woman slumped on the ground, groaning. As I bent down to her, she asked me to call 911. I assumed she was lost, a probable detox patient from a nearby residential drug rehabilitation center, and I immediately phoned them to report finding her. They confirmed that she had wandered off and would come and get her. While we waited, the young woman suddenly became violently sick and began to vomit uncontrollably. She broke into hot sweats and began to cry. At this point, I rubbed her back and accessed the three gateways, placing my attention on the inner energy field of the body and my long, deep breaths. At one point, between retching spells, the woman whispered barely audibly, "Wow, I really feel better. You should come and work at the center. We could really use you over there."

Smiling, I immediately recognized the woman's appearance at my doorstep as the manifestation of my earlier resolve to simply be of service, in the moment, without desire for a "bigger" payoff produced by the awakening process. There we were, simply being together in the moment, allowing presence to flow through me into her. The needs of the manuscript on my laptop and no author role could usurp or take precedence over this simple expression of service presented by the river of life in the moment. Then, when the manager of the rehab center arrived to pick the woman up, she noted the woman's sudden revival and thanked me profusely and offered me a job, stating that she could really use someone "just like you."

Once your coveted roles are identified, the fuel that once served to uphold them can now be funneled to maintaining a sustained peace or even of attaining enlightenment. Once a more peaceful state arises in you, your perspective then naturally aligns with right motivation and right action. Ironically, stress from scrabbling for goal completion is absent as the present moment itself is appreciated and allowed to flow naturally and to produce whatever is helpful.

Sometimes, one of our coveted roles is deleted by the universe without our having to excise it ourselves. When this happens, we are saved from having to wrench it out from under us with the force of our own spiritual practice. Sometimes this is when we get fired, become laid off, injured, or lose "things," for any possible reason. (In spiritual literature, this is sometimes referred to as the "Divine Boot.") If this has happened, rejoice. You are living your spiritual practice for real, with the universe's cooperation, and your potential gains are enormous.

In the early days of Jeannette's disease, her husband may have unconsciously attempted to deal with the sad news of her condition by sustaining an extraordinary workload. Probably, at some point, he must have ignored the universe's input to slow down, or to go more deeply inside in order to more consciously face his and her unfolding ordeal. Instead, he barreled on, carrying an enormous caseload and extensive traveling, all of which may have exhausted him, physically and mentally. Thus, it was no surprise, from a spiritual perspective, when he hurt his back, requiring him to immediately stop his horrendous schedule and stay home to heal.

In the event that you are currently at a crisis point in your life where an item on your list is actually being threatened, through loss, death, or for any reason, then congratulations are offered. Your spiritual homework has begun in earnestness. There is no intention here to be flippant; however, there is no benefit to upholding the myth that the timing of the ebb and flow of the river of life is accidental. It's recognized that every single social, business, and familial convention in society supports this myth, which thereby includes most unawakened humans on the planet. This myth is unraveling as an unsupportable falsehood that cannot stand up to the light of truth.

Sink into the feeling of loss. Recognize that something mysterious conspired to get you to this exact point. Here you are, minus that role, and it is painful. Allow the grief of it to be there, but don't make a story out of it. Don't resist it. Just observe the grief in you, as though you are an innocent bystander observing a third person. Don't judge the grief; allow it to be there for now. Of its own, it will work its way up and through you, until the pain dissolves.

There are few more potent opportunities for growth than to have outward circumstances snatch away one of your most cherished identities. Suddenly, there's a panic when something or someone you've identified strongly with is suddenly gone. When the comfortable belief in your main source of happiness or well-being virtually vanishes, fear can emerge like a monster emerging from a lake; however, this is your opportunity. This is your Titanic event, during which the sinking of a cherished false role, form, or identity can lead you straight to yourself. Once sunk, as occurred with my author role, they may, if supported by life, bubble back up to the surface, but now newly aligned with presence.

For those who have no immediate loss occurring—meaning you are not unemployed, or your kids are not causing you heartache, or your dog isn't dying—your entries won't offer the same degree of punch of those already in the throes of a catastrophe. But, whether you apply this practice with or without benefit of the actual loss, apply it you must if you wish to dissolve your strongest identifications in preparation for living a more awakened life. Now armed with sufficient motivation to conduct a thorough inspection of your ego's domain, your ego will no longer run you ragged with its shallow interpretation of what's needed for happiness. Now, *you,* your powerful true essence, which has been covered up far too long, can finally prevail.

In my case, it was a bonus of indescribable worth to be unemployed after resigning my position as office manager at the surgical practice. To reduce my identity down to its simplest component, wherein I cancelled my cell phone plan, health insurance, gym membership, and was told that I was ineligible for unemployment insurance, was startling. Suddenly, a hundred dollars was a lot of money.

This was when I had no choice but to surrender to my circumstances, and to more deeply sink into the depths of myself. Loss can be a great motivator for spiritual practice. Suffering as a result of loss can reduce mental resistance in refusing to accept what cannot be accepted. This truth was just barely sinking in, as I sat under the palm tree with Eckhart Tolle's books, prior to the river of life spilling me onto the shore of Jeannette's home.

Initially, in keeping with the dysfunction of the egoic mind, when the position was offered to me, my mind squeaked out an objection, saying that I was capable of managing an entire medical practice of sick people, not just one woman. Even Jeannette's husband, at the time of our interview, was concerned and asked me, "Aren't you overqualified?" But even back then, I had already begun to suspect that just because a thought enters my mind doesn't mean that it's true.

To finally recognize that all thoughts need to be questioned as to their veracity with respect to spiritual truth, a new possibility for me arose. Fortunately, I ignored all the egoic mental noise, and I accepted the position as an opportunity for growth. That willingness to question the inherent truth of my thoughts and to accept a more humble position was the difference between the old me and enlightenment. Had I allowed my mind to talk me out of it with its litany of reasons, who knows how many further diversions would have occurred before my awakening? While another opportunity would have eventually presented itself, given a choice to awaken right now or next decade, I'll take the present moment. My willingness to recognize the nature of my mental objection to a simpler job than I expected produced a deep trust that the river of life was supporting me in realizing the truest goal of my soul: enlightenment.

Now that we have explored the way that entrenched "roles" can sabotage the uncovering of presence, let's move on to the next category, to that of "Forms."

## Identify Cherished "Forms"

It is ironic in the extreme that had I not, following the loss of so much of my "stuff" when I left my Malibu ranch, continued to uphold a simpler material lifestyle, I would not have so seamlessly stepped into my position as Jeannette's caregiver. For the first time in decades, I had no pets or young children for which I was responsible, and my general state of affairs was a vastly more pared-down existence. Otherwise, my ability to work long hours and to devote my full attention to Jeannette would have been significantly curtailed. By unloading so much of my previous stuff, I was fundamentally more focused on living a deeper, more meaningful life, spiritually speaking. Thus, my new, less-complicated lifestyle enabled me to deal better with my DP.

The "Forms" column is relatively straightforward. Simply identify all the stuff that you have worked very hard to obtain or maintain that secretly upholds, adds to, or strengthens your image. In addition, even if it doesn't uphold an image, identify your stuff that you say you "can't live without."

As I was filling in my own list in the "Forms" column, I became aware of the fact that, as I aged, I was increasing the frequency of my appointments at my hair salon because I loathed the gray and white hair that was replacing my red hair. In addition, although initially I believed that having long hair was simply a preference, I came to admit that it was actually a cherished demand. For example, if the hair stylist accidentally trimmed too much, I didn't like it because I wanted long hair. It wasn't that the stylist would trim six inches instead of a quarter inch; it was that I noticed internal objection if she trimmed a quarter inch instead of an eighth of an inch. Prior to this exercise, I just took it for granted that each of us has preferences. But upon closer inspection, I recognized that my cherished preferences and opinions are not really just that. Instead, they often have become full-blown identities. In essence, I was attached to my hair and spent a great deal of time thinking about it and coloring it. So, under the "Forms" column, I added the entry, "Long hair that has no gray showing," a form to which I had an enormous identification.

As I continued with part two of this practice, during which I was to imagine its disappearance, I decided to take a literal approach and do the heretofore unthinkable, cutting it all off and making it *short*. Henceforth, I decided that there would be no more coloring it. Over the course of the next year, I received many comments from friends about how terrible my hair looked. This was enormously instructive, and I began to find it quite humorous that, although my hair identification had dissolved in *me*, it was still alive in *them* on my behalf. Funnily enough, after completing a hundred-day fast, some of my hair actually fell out, which produced an opportunity to meditate on having no hair at all. Then, as if to reward me for such a thorough dis-identification with my hair, it actually grew back in with my original hair color, strawberry blond. Then, the same friends who had disapproved of my graying hair, now applauded me for coming around to their way of thinking and coloring it again, which I assured them I didn't do. Currently, my hair appears to be mostly strawberry blond, with some gray and white, but in the future, should it again turn all gray or white, there will be no attempt to salvage it with hair color to uphold a younger identity.

Other examples of forms that you may be thoroughly identified with are: your new sports car; your team's season tickets; your big house; your toned, fit body; or your too thin or too heavy body, etc. You will know if any particular form has become an identity because the existence of it causes you to feel superior (or inferior) to others. If you secretly get any kind of egoic satisfaction from noticing that you have it and others often do not, then add it to your list. This means that to qualify as an entry, you have to look deeply and courageously to determine if the "thing" in question brings with it—no matter how silly or shallow—an ego boost when in comparison with others. Often, this ego boost can be very subtle, and unless there is astute self-awareness, you may not even recognize this tendency within yourself.

Also, and equally as important, it's essential to explore the reverse side of the coin, meaning investigate bodily deficits, because anything to do with body image, whether positive or negative, is all borne from egoic thought. Although we normally consider ego to mean ideas of "better-than-you," it is also responsible for thoughts of poor self-esteem or shyness. Because the ego is looking for ways to prove that you should be gloating or suffering from any offense, it will either construct a false identity made of shallow means to feel better, or it will magnify anything to explain why you feel bad or inferior—as evidenced by your deficit.

This means, that if you have a poor self-image due to extra weight or any kind of physical or apparent material imperfection, this poor self-image is also created from the egoic thought structure. As a result, you must include on your list those entries that, if you could never rid yourself of it or be able to correct it, would cause upset. So for the chronically overweight person, who truly believes that losing weight will make them feel better, add "excess body weight" to your list. Then, in the second part, you don't imagine the disappearance of the excess weight, but rather, you imagine the disappearance of achieving the loss of the excess weight. This will allow you to find your true essence right now, without need of gaining any "future" accomplishment in order to feel at peace.

Many Asian women, and certainly many women in any culture, believe that their breasts are too small. An extraordinary amount of women's attention is placed on this one area of the body. Of course, both genders have their potential areas of dysfunctional focus, and so both genders must be courageous in fully completing their lists. In any case, women and men can identify and then add to their list those body parts that their egoic mind structure has convinced them is "wrong."

For example, as a young woman in my early twenties, I was a television commercial actress who represented various products in varying environments. If lucky enough to ace the audition and actually shoot the commercial, then I hoped it went national, meaning that the commercial played widely on many television stations and enjoyed broad coverage. When this happened, residual checks arrived in the mail. Sometimes, one good television commercial could yield a tidy sum in weekly residuals for a year or longer.

In any case, I had done several commercials, including one for Levi's in which I was "costumed" in a low-cut halter top complete with leather tassels and beads and was the driver of an enormous Harley Davidson motorbike. Another female model was placed behind me facing backwards, and together we were filmed racing through the streets of downtown San Francisco, wearing our tight Levi jeans.

As a result of this commercial, including the fact that my then boyfriend preferred a well-endowed woman, I decided that my breasts were too small. Soon after, I scheduled an appointment with a plastic surgeon in order to correct this mistake of nature. Today, I can only laugh at the way that my egoic thought structure had so railroaded me that it successfully dictated breast surgery in an attempt to improve two parts of my body. Obviously, this is a prime example of a strong identification with form.

When it comes to completing the "Forms" column on your list, be courageous and identify all those areas about which you are secretly offended or embarrassed, in addition to those that you believe help your image. In so doing, it is the first step in becoming aware that any kind of offense taken—whether being offended by a DP or by some personal characteristic—is still sponsored by egoic thought. Remember, that's what the mind does, it finds fault. That's why it's important, as described throughout this book, when you *do* properly identify areas of mental dysfunction, *do not judge it*—or the ego has gone down one road, but has come back up on the other. "Wrongness" and "badness" are labels that are dispensed by a noisy, egoic thought structure. Be aware of this as you complete your list.

The purpose of this exercise is to find areas of faulty identification that make up your false identity, whether or not those are considered positive roles, forms, or attributes or negative ones. Self-realization involves the dissolving of all false identities, but you can't consciously dissolve them if you deny their existence. So be vigilant and add all those habits of self-critiquing to the appropriate column on your list.

## Identify Cherished "Attributes"

Once you have completed both the "Roles" and the "Forms" columns, begin filling in the "Attributes" column. As can be expected, this is where you will add all those abilities or enhancements of yours, whether they are athletic, professional, or sexual, and those of appearance, stylishness, or a cultured "taste," etc., that can be identified as providing egoic satisfaction. Identify those attributes that you consider to be developed in you to a higher degree than in most people, which may or may not give you an inflated sense of yourself. Only you know whether an attribute is a sticking point, spiritually speaking. If you can catch yourself feeling superior as a result of it, then add it to your list. If you can catch the way you've become attached to it by virtue of your embarrassment when it is not with you or not part of you, then add that to your list. For example, if you identify yourself as someone who has great fashion sense, but you also recognize that you would "die" if someone caught you at home in the garden wearing overalls, then add "fashionista" to your list; however, please recognize that the exercise is not designed to flatter you. Instead, you are courageously identifying those areas in which you feel superior to others, so that you can then excise them.

Putting it another way, for example, if someone gives you a compliment about your muscles, and you feel a little blown up by it and are inspired by the compliment to work out with more fervor, you have stumbled upon an identification. Add it to your list. Of course, there is nothing wrong with muscles, stylish clothes, shiny cars, and big houses. We are merely attempting to identify those roles, forms, and attributes that have become an identity, which means that your ego has become attached to it and has used it as a way to blow you and it up in comparison with others. This blown-up, false part of you stands in the way of true humility, which is one of the characteristics of a being who does not stand out as significant by virtue of any of the usual worldly determinations. As foreign a concept as this may seem to you, we are entering new ground inasmuch as the way of the spiritual seeker is the opposite to that of the ego's path.

As I contemplated all the areas in which I felt egoic superiority to others, I stumbled upon the realization that my sense of healthy eating and my preference for frequenting gourmet health food stores had become a virtual identity of mine. When this was recognized, I delved deeper and saw that I had created an entire identify around my consumption of health foods, vegan products, and organic food. Of course, there is nothing wrong with taking vitamins and preferring foods without pesticides. Many people have developed an entire identity around the concept of having a finer palette than others, and as such, refer to themselves as a "foodie." The emphasis here is on noticing in what areas of life you have developed an identity, and recognizing when that identity is used to feel superior or special. Then, when I further considered this area of food, I recognized a tendency to identify food itself as a means to gain serenity. Although food is a "form," I arrived at the conclusion while investigating identifications within the "attributes" category. But this doesn't matter. However you are able to follow a thread to an ever-deepening awareness of your egoic tendencies, simply follow it courageously until fully explored.

When I recognized this strong identity to achieve serenity through food, I consciously began to pay attention to the nature of my thoughts whenever I consumed anything. As a result of this exploration, I began an extended supervised fast, wherein I consumed only clear, strained vegetable and fruit juices to include liquid vitamins. After successfully completing a 100-day fast while working full-time as caregiver, I had thoroughly examined the way and manner of how I had previously used food as a means to dissolve anxiety. Once fully examined, any false identification tends to then become very obvious, and it dissolves on its own. When presence is "added" through accessing the three gateways, while simultaneously meditating upon the second part of this exercise, an easier deepening naturally occurs.

While on my extended fast, I had reason to be part of a group of other fasters. What I discovered was that the fasters developed particularly strong identifications to their role as a "person who can fast a long time." Of course, they did not recognize their new alignment with this identity. Many reported the relief of being free of the identification with food, at least temporarily; however, it takes great insight to recognize a replacement of one identity with another. This is the case with many vegetarians and vegans, wherein they feel a sense of superiority with respect to food choices and the proclaimed "gentler" way of living and eating. It is commonplace for vegetarians and vegans to feel that they live far more spiritually centered lives because of their meatless diet, which ensures that they are "eating their way to heaven." But in actual fact, it is far more spiritually telling to pay close attention to what is coming *out* of the mouth, rather than what's going *in* it. Are your *words* almost entirely comprised of negatives: complaints, judgments, and comments about others' inferior characteristics or your disapproval of circumstances and events? Can you catch the frequency of your secret thoughts that have to do with your superiority based on your diet? As you can see, developing a keen observation of what goes on in the *mind* is far more potentially transformative than a compulsive focus on what goes in the *mouth*. The damage done by a noisy mind in savaging others through chronic, secret criticism of their lifestyle or just garden-variety superiority, is far more negative and produces far more environmental toxicity than does any meat eater. Vegetarians often claim to be living a more spiritual life than their meat-eating counterparts based on their "gentler" food choices, but a vegetarian's food choice does not at all equate to a more gentle quality of their thoughts. If you are a vegan or vegetarian, you may as well add this to your list because it is highly unusual for those identified with this "role" to have escaped chronic feelings of superiority to nonvegans/vegetarians.

At a recent event where I attended a lecture by Eckhart Tolle, an audience member seemed surprised at the answer to her question when she asked Tolle's girlfriend if she or Tolle eats meat. Kim Eng, an awakened spiritual teacher herself, replied that both of them eat meat, and in fact eat "everything," although in moderation. Tolle, the absolute embodiment of a gentle, peaceful way of living, has transformed his own life and the lives of millions of his readers worldwide. Yet what is his focus? A quiet *mind* arrived at by focusing on *nothing*, rather than improvements in diet or appearance or any other kind of "enhancement." The same is true for the Dalai Lama, the spiritual leader of Tibet and a world-renowned spiritual teacher who attracts enormous crowds wherever he speaks. Although once a vegetarian, he now eats meat but continues to focus on the importance of upholding a nonjudgmental, humble, and therefore peaceful, existence. Conversely, some vegetarians and vegans, convinced that their food choices make them more spiritual, in fact may often demonstrate an extremely noisy mind, which virtually guarantees that they are producing suffering for themselves and others.

Egoic superiority, for whatever reason, and a loud, noisy mind are very evident and can be detected from afar. Further, it is precisely this dance of the ego that makes enlightenment, or even a more peaceful existence, impossible. For any long-time vegan or vegetarian yogi, this may come as a surprise; however, the dense energetic frequency that surrounds hidden feelings and secret thoughts of egoic superiority is palpable and reduces presence's power, rather than uncovers it. Whatever strong, egoic identification is present—whether of a proclaimed "gentle" practice or not—it is still an identification as sponsored by the egoic mind structure. These are usually the most difficult to detect because such people already assume their own superiority, and thus are less likely to find evidence of false attachments. So be courageous. If you have not achieved a mostly peaceful existence, or as a spiritual practitioner have not awakened spiritually but have been on the path a long time, you might want to meditate upon the strength of your remaining egoic identifications, even if they are aligned with a so-called spiritual way of life.

The beauty of effective spiritual practice, when you access the three gateways and dissolve your cherished identifications, is that once you experience the blissful deepening that a quiet mind uncovers, you choose to have more of it. Once tasted, peace and well-being are not easily traded for judgment and negativity; being habitually offended by this or that and cherishing roles, forms, and attributes to that degree causes suffering. This is the point at which spiritual practice is clearly recognized as producing its own rewards. You won't need to coerce yourself to put into place that which produces immediate and demonstrable results. If there is any challenge at all, it's your concern for less mature "finders" who have not given the practice a chance to uncover the bliss that they so desperately seek. What you would be missing is having the indescribable sweetness of your true essence uncovered by virtue of the diminishment of mental chatter and strong egoic identifications to that of roles, forms, and attributes.

From afar, effective spiritual practice may seem like one more chore to be done, one more boring or tedious thing to add to the "to do" list. Unlike meditation, which can produce frustration at the inability to quiet the mind, or even when the mind *is* quieted, eventually, one must bring an effective spiritual practice out of the meditation room and into daily life.

It is common for lifelong meditators to have as chronically noisy minds as someone who's never meditated. It's ironic that, just because an hour of successful meditation was achieved, doesn't necessarily mean that you're on a "spiritual path." If you then go out in the world and cannot tolerate the dynamics of your own family or work environment, it's time to look more closely at your mental patterns. If a quiet mind does not begin to seep into familial relationships and work environments and if you are not nearing at least part-time well-being, then your mediation, yoga practice, etc., is not that effective. Ultimately, of course, at the heart of such practices is the goal of quieting the mind, but often this becomes lost in daily life when replaced with outer body focus. No amount of flexibility or thinking about quieting the mind will produce a quiet mind. Long-time yoga students, for example, do not necessarily acquire any more spiritual maturity than the average person if there is not an arising recognition of the true obstacle to awakening: compulsive thinking. Because a strong identification with an entrenched role can serve to bolster the ego, not diminish it, a meditator or a yogi's ego can be thus strengthened. When you are able to quiet the mind for an hour daily and include letting go of the ways that you hold secret superiority through identifications, the next step is to bring that practice into all the interpersonal relationships and dynamics of daily living.

If you've been consulting with an expert financial advisor for a decade, but you're bankrupt, it's time to change experts. In the same way, if you've been practicing a particular spiritual practice or have been consulting with myriad spiritual consultants, teachers, or therapists, and your degree of well-being is decreasing rather than increasing, you might want to rethink your current program. It takes great insight and wisdom to identify less than effective spiritual practices and spiritual teachers, and this is because the mind works very hard at ensuring that no inroads are made in the direction of an arising awakening. If your *mind* approves heartily of your spiritual teacher, he or she may not be that well grounded in presence.

The ego thought structure is loathe to tolerate quiet and effective spiritual practice that obliterates it. So take note of your current program, and consider you may have turned it into a crutch, rather than an instrument to ensure spiritual growth. Spiritual teachers or therapists are only helpful if they help you to uncover your inner presence that is already there but perhaps quite obscured. If they even subtly support you with remaining in a stance of objection to family members, friends, and coworkers or your own life circumstances, then you have been assisted in denying the recognition of your own worst enemy: your own dysfunctional mental patterns.

If you cannot see your difficult family member's dysfunctional mental patterns alive in you, too, then you are still sleeping, spiritually speaking. Becoming dependent on a spiritual teacher or therapist is not helpful to your growth. Whatever dependence you may have initially developed must, over time, be decreasing, not increasing. If not, then you might want to take a look at who is benefiting from that dependence. There is nothing wrong with teachers and therapists, so long as a dependent relationship is not fostered in which your growth has been unconsciously thwarted. Of course, mind-dominated therapists and spiritual teachers are common, so choose wisely. If you want to know the effectiveness of your teacher or therapist, observe the degree of their encouragement of you recognizing and then unraveling identification with false images and becoming aware of the symptoms of a chronically noisy mind. Only a wise teacher will ever help you notice how your own mental patterns are probably quite similar to that of your "enemy"—your father who rubs you the wrong way, your hated neighbor who verbally attacks you, your sister who sometimes irritates you, or your friend who is "getting under your skin."

Any effective spiritual practice must assist you in noticing how frequently you become offended by others, virtually without ceasing. Although you may have labeled this habit as being "sensitive," there's actually nothing sensitive about it at all. True sensitivity involves recognizing that your own misguided mental patterns are, most likely, virtually identical to those who offend you. Habitual reaction to others' comments and actions is, instead, *reactionary* and in fact is quite *in*sensitive. If you must react, at least call it what it is: resistance extraordinaire.

This is why it is so important to recognize that, despite being in the midst of difficult people and difficult problems, a spiritual ripening can absolutely occur if you elevate effective spiritual practice to a priority within a context of everyday challenges and activities. You *can* awaken, spiritually, in your own household if you courageously observe your own noisy mental patterns. Your problems and the difficult people who surround you all point to the road to freedom.

As you continue exploring your identification to attributes, you may notice that the flipside to "attribute" is a "deficit." This means that your list is not complete unless you also include those areas that you feel are your bad qualities. Chronic illness, disease, handicap of any kind, or a bad reputation for any reason often hinder your ability to fully embrace your true worth as the lovely essence that is life. With respect to so-called "deficits," these can include physical abnormalities that have to do with the physical body, or they can include intangible deficits such as the negative reputation incurred from past mistakes or errors.

Let's first discuss the deficits involving the physical body. As was already mentioned, when the mind returns to a problem again and again that has to do with the physical body, the egoic mind is still operating strongly. Simply become aware of this, and once identified, allow your meditation to bring better awareness of how your ego has used your illness or pain as a means to keep a noisy mind, and thus a cherished identification, intact. As you proceed to the second part of the exercise wherein you meditate on the disappearance of it, remember to focus on the disappearance of the *hope* or future possibility that it may disappear and cease to be a problem for you. The idea is to stop needing a future in order to be at peace. Whatever the problem, meditate on the recognition that you now understand that it's here to stay, but it doesn't matter and does not need to affect your ability to feel chronically peaceful. While meditating, remember to focus on the breath and the inner energy field of the body as you visualize your "deficit."

In my case, I had recognized a very strong identification with a familial hereditary condition involving the cause of nosebleeds and other sources of extensive bleeding. Unchecked, the condition can be fatal—surprising, considering that the person may be in otherwise excellent health. Even a relatively young person in great health, when diagnosed with HHT (Hereditary Hemorrhagic Telangiectasia), can suddenly "bleed out" and be in a life-threatening situation. Because a young relative of mine had suddenly died from this condition, and because it is present in my genealogy, I had many opportunities to observe the way that strong identifications to physical conditions cause an actual *strengthening* of the egoic structure.

As a result, I have been keenly aware of the underlying mechanics of these types of identifications to illnesses or conditions, and as such, have refrained from taking it on as an identity, despite my own intermittent, severe nosebleeds. Although many people assume that medical conditions would contribute to underlying poor self-esteem, this is not the case for the egoic mind structure. Instead, like everything else that it co-opts for its own enhancement, health problems can serve to significantly strengthen the identification to false roles. Like an errant yet ignored grade-schooler, any attention is better than no attention, and the pain body rejoices at another opportunity to feed. Anytime a medical diagnosis is rendered, the student of spirituality must be vigilant in resisting the pain body's attraction to the diagnosis in using it to bolster itself. You will know the pain body has succeeded when you catch yourself repeatedly talking about your condition, because it causes physical discomfort or challenges. By their very definition, identifications are designed to strengthen the pain body, for the simple reason that *all identifications* are created by the ego, for the ego.

Several years ago, I was giving a talk to an audience at the Bodhi Tree bookstore in Los Angeles. During my presentation, my nose began to bleed severely. Unlike most normal nosebleeds where you simply put your head back and await the blood clotting, HHT nosebleeds often do not stop for quite a while. It's not unusual to require large beach towels, instead of tissue, while awaiting coagulation. In any event, during this particular public speaking event, I did not take a break during the nosebleed, despite some very concerned participants. Continuing with the presentation, a huge wad of tissue was provided, and I carried on, unaffected. Although the sight of a lot of blood can be disconcerting to others, it is not to me. Simply because you may have been diagnosed with a life-threatening illness or condition does not at all mean that you must identify with it.

By using my underlying HHT condition as part of this spiritual practice, I was not only able to dis-identify from any unconscious attachment to the condition, but also to surrender to it as the cause of my own imagined death during the second part of this exercise. While using this particular condition as a way to imagine the process of "bleeding out" and then observing my own rotting corpse, any fear of anemia or death as a result of HHT became nonexistent.

Use whatever underlying physical limitation or condition you have as a means to surrender to the perfection of life, just as it is. When you consciously, through your deep meditation, allow all of your attachments and strong identifications to roles, forms, and attributes to die away, they lose their ability to produce fear of their loss in you. Once you have relinquished all your "stuff" back to dust, then you, too, can return home, confident that you were always there anyway. By "dying while alive," you are reborn.

8

# The Hybrid

THE PROCESS OF MY spiritual awakening coincided with Jeannette's increasingly intensifying pain body as she reacted to the loss of her driver's license and ability to write checks and complete ordinary household tasks. The more angry and difficult she became, the more disciplined I became as I observed mental patterns that we actually shared. At first, if she demonstrated frustration at a garbage truck blocking the road by yelling and slamming her hand on the dashboard, I would then become internally frustrated with her outburst. But then suddenly I got it: both behaviors were identical. Her impatience or gritty intolerance of life's ups and downs could be observed as alive in me too, as I responded to *her* temper tantrums with judgmental thoughts. She resisted *something*, and then I resisted *her*. "*Amazing,*" I realized.

One day the clarity of this mirror reflection almost blinded me. It was as though a laser beam was shot from the heavens and blasted me with full comprehension: Each of our mental patterns in this kind of interaction is virtually identical. The only trouble is, you may acknowledge your own misguided patterns but deny that they are as pronounced as the other person's. There's a repetitive pattern of denial as you point to the other person saying, "Look at his terrible behavior! I'm not perfect, but I'm not as bad as *he* is!" Even so, that fact wouldn't make your patterns any *less* misguided, just not *as* misguided. The underlying framework of your mutual defects is virtually identical.

When awakening occurs, the mind's role diminishes in importance as a perspective shift occurs from "outer" to "inner." Whereas once you solely observed others' nuances, now you observe your own. The mind's compulsive need to think becomes subordinate to *you*. This is the glorious shift that imbues this new state of being with boundless space. Whereas what was once a humanoid—with a predictably dysfunctional mind, used for predictably dysfunctional purposes, compelled to arrive at predictably intolerant conclusions, producing predictable conflict and strife—now emerges on the scene a reengineered human hybrid. This new human, whose predecessor was subject to the back-and-forth pull of negative drama and the pain body waltz, now is "reworked" with an orientation toward peace and peaceful solutions.

The process to enlightenment signals that a hybrid is born, which is the best of both worlds: a human who has a mind and can still think and align with their essence to *solve* problems, but whose mind doesn't *cause* problems. This hybrid cherishes stillness and peace above all else and recognizes that everyone, like themselves, is actually comprised of this stillness and peace as their essence. That's why everyone seems so loveable to them. The difficult person, previously not recognized as your "partner in crime," is now observed to be traveling the same path that you once did. Now, rather than judging him for stumbling on the ruts on the road, you make a gentle practice of pointing out just where those ruts are.

The hybrid relishes the ever-present melody of stillness in the background, sometimes quite loud and other times, a lovely whisper. Sometimes this melody of stillness is subdued, but it is always very present, nonetheless. A compulsive need to search for problems drops away as the hybrid's new orientation toward peace very naturally flourishes. They are no longer *of* this world; the hybrid is *in* it. They are not part of *form* but part of *space*, looking at the form with no objections to it. Of course, you were always part of space, but once awakened, you *know* that you will never again misconstrue your identification with form. Now aligned with the simplicity of essence, the hybrid's simplicity of being emerges to everyone's benefit.

The mind can still be picked up and used to think in the present moment, but it is done so lightly. It is used as a tool and then put back down. Thought no longer runs deeply in a misguided fashion through the core of this being, so the mind ceases causing problems and destruction.

Thought takes its place as a secondary instrument to essence that well serves the hybrid's creative expression, no matter which professional or personal goals are sought. Indeed, once awakened, the hybrids unfurl often with extreme bursts of creativity, since all their once-trapped energy is now entirely available for creative expression. In the same way that a bottle of seltzer water, after being shaken and uncorked, explodes as a geyser; once the hybrid's storehouse of energies becomes available for use, myriad expressions of creativity are borne. However, these energies now serve and are aligned with the river of life, rather than serving the squall of the ego.

After awakening, everything from visiting a grocery store to driving an often-traveled road feels new, as though experienced for the first time. Even though I had visited a country store in Malibu thousands of times since childhood, the experience of walking its aisles was fresh and new. The experience of this is miraculous, and does produce some degree of initial disorientation as something new has arisen within the old, familiar environment. The eyes look out at the world in a different way. Also, because the mind actually functions differently, I became aware of how it's actually somewhat difficult to think of the past and future. It's as though, once a new orientation occurs in aligning with the present moment, the mind doesn't go to the past or the future so easily. Through stable alignment with the present moment is initially disorienting, it's a feeling that's a pleasure to experience and is more accurately a *re*-orientation: a corrected, more aligned way of being.

The awakened being sees rightly for the first time without the heavy veil of thought clouding interpretation. There is a marked reduction in needing to name that which is being observed. Previously the mind would compare and contrast with the compulsion of a gambler, but when the mind takes second place to essence, those secret, savage thoughts of comparison and criticism fall away. In its place, gentle observation occurs without the need to chronically find evidence of superiority. Instead, evidence of beauty and loveliness are observed everywhere. The swoop of a pelican's low gleaming body, just inches from the glassy ocean, produces an explosion of compassion and utter disbelief at the sheer perfection of life.

Spiritual practice enables the inner energy field of the body to become fully available, as Kundalini energy rises up the spine and flows freely. Kundalini energy is the natural energy of the true self and lies dormant at the base of the spine until it awakens. When spiritual development and expanding awareness occur, its energy is made available as a great reservoir of creative force. It is experienced as extreme energy rushes that are quick and forceful. As Kundalini energy ignites with the inner energy field of the body, a powerful door to awakening opens. This energy continues to flow unheeded through the hybrid, creating a useable vessel through which heightened life force can express itself.

Many months prior to my actual burst of awakening, it was evident to me that my own pain body was mostly dissolved. That's how I knew that my impending enlightenment was close, because an indescribable, unchanging peace and chronic sense of well-being rarely left me. It was made known to me that my awakening would happen over a three-month period, culminating in August 2010. Right on schedule following three months of intensive processing, a burst of awakening did occur, which deepened over the course of the week and the next few months.

On the very day I was "scheduled" to awaken, I accompanied Jeannette and her family on vacation to Maui. Awaking at midnight for the hour drive to the Haleakala Volcano, Jeannette's daughter and I travelled uphill to the summit, which rises to 10,000 feet above sea level. I was intuitively drawn to the habitat of the Ohi'a trees—the quintessential endemic Hawaiian plant. They are reported to be among the oldest flowering plants on Earth. Humanity's evolution to an enlightened state can be considered as analogous to the first flowering plants on the planet. This is the "flowering of human consciousness," as Tolle refers to it. In other words, if you can imagine the magnificence of the very first time a plant flowered, this began a new phase of breathtaking evolution with plant life on Earth; enlightenment, too, promises a similar explosion of loveliness. When humanity dissolves that part of itself that creates strife, the thorns of our personalities dissolve, leaving the soft pastels of our potential. Analogously, where once was a thicket of tumbleweeds, gerbera daisies and orange poppies can now proliferate.

In addition to being drawn to the locale of the Ohi'a trees, Haleakala Volcano itself was an additional destination site for me. The Hawaiian Islands are located within the Pacific Ring of Fire, an area where large numbers of earthquakes and volcanic eruptions occur in the basin of the Pacific Ocean. The Pacific Ring of Fire is a 25,000-mile horseshoe-shaped crescent and is associated with a nearly continuous series of oceanic trenches, volcanic arcs, volcanic belts, and plate movements. It has 452 volcanoes, and because volcanoes are not randomly distributed over the Earth's surface, the Pacific Ring of Fire alone is home to 75 percent of the world's active and dormant volcanoes. The Hawaiian Islands lie within this crescent.

There is a stunning parallel relationship between the "awakening" process of the Kundalini energy as it comes alive within the human body at the time of enlightenment and the geothermal energy flow that finds its way to the surface of the earth via volcanoes. Kundalini is the life force that resides at the base of the spine until it is activated by effective spiritual practice and it moves up the spine to the head. The Kundalini energy flows within a human being who is awakening spiritually is a microcosm of the greater energy flow occurring within our mother host, Planet Earth. The Earth's macrocosmic geothermal energy flows and humans' microcosmic Kundalini energy flows are deeply interconnected, and as such, can be demonstrated to intermingle and conspire in fuelling the awakening process. For a student of spirituality, and a finder who is ripe, these converging energies can be tapped with explosive results.

Consider the following "outer" macrocosm as it relates to an "inner" microcosm with respect to these two converging energy flows:

*Volcanoes serve as a way for geothermal energy to find its way to the surface of the earth.*

*The inner energy field of the body and the breath serve as a gateway for stillness so that Kundalini energy can find its way and rise up through your body to the surface of your head.*

*Geothermal energy is heat from the center of the earth.*
*Kundalini energy is stillness from the center of your body.*

*Geothermal energy is a sleeping, dormant potential force in the earthly organism.*
*Kundalini energy is a sleeping, dormant potential force in the human organism.*

*Naturally occurring large areas of hydrothermal resources are called geothermal reservoirs.*
*Naturally occurring large areas of "stillness" resources are called Kundalini reservoirs.*

*Geothermals are the energies of the earth that reside within the Pacific Ring of Fire, and elsewhere, until it is aroused.*
*Kundalini is the energy of consciousness that resides within the sleeping body until it is aroused.*

*Most of the geothermal activity in the world occurs amidst the Pacific Ring of Fire.*
*Most of the enlightenment activity in the world occurs amidst effective spiritual practice.*

From my perspective as a lifelong "experiencer" of extraterrestrial contact phenomena, exposure to extreme otherworldly phenomena induced an acute sensitivity in me to readily sense energies, both geothermal and Kundalini. Although this sensitivity is not required for awakening, it is extremely helpful in allowing me to articulate this energetic convergence to you so that you can put into place effective spiritual practice. Once implemented, you *can* increase your sensitivity and exposure to these energies, and thus allow your natural state to be uncovered so that enlightenment can occur.

Watching the sunrise over the rim of the crater on that miraculous morning, energies conspired to further activate both Kundalini and geothermal sensitivities in me. This activation is palpable and can produce dramatic physiological reactions such as dizziness, glassy eyes, nausea, and disorientation, not to be confused with altitude sickness. It is accompanied by a profound inner peace. A person so affected can be easily mistaken for someone who is intoxicated. In fact, Jeannette's daughter, while taking photographs of me, was laughing and saying, "You look drunk. Blissful, but drunk." In my case, these symptoms lasted for a couple months and as of this writing are either reduced, or it simply feels that way because it has become my normal state, and as such, is ongoing. Every time I travel to an area that is very geographically alive with seismic activity or geothermal energies, I reexperience the identical deep bliss and feeling of intense euphoria. During such times, others frequently ask me if there is something wrong, because I seem "out of it."

Upon departing Maui two days later, I arrived in Vancouver, Canada, the northeastern boundary of the Pacific Ring of Fire. Extremely sensitive to the arising of both Kundalini energy within my body, as well as the arising geothermal energies in my environment, the next day I attended Eckhart Tolle's taping for his web-based TV show, barely able to contain my nausea, dizziness, and joy upon beholding *his* energetic countenance.

The human body's physiological movement toward the

expression of spiritual enlightenment matches the intense global, seismic, and volcanic activity alive within the Pacific Ring of Fire and elsewhere on Earth. Whether or not Eckhart Tolle considered this when posing his gateways to the now—the inner energy field of the human body, the breath, and the present moment—they are deeply analogous to Earth's "inner" geothermal energies that lie still and dormant until becoming activated through volcanic activity. The three gateways, like geothermal energies, lie unsuspectingly asleep until activated through effective spiritual practice.

We have already explored the way that the inner energy field of the body, the breath, and the present moment are at their essence a pure creative force. It's remarkable when we consider that the magma flowing up lava tubes from the Earth's mantle is what creates volcanoes and, along with its gases, are quite literally a pure creative force that helped form the Earth's first oceans and its atmosphere. This means that without volcanic magma and its gases, human life on Earth would not be possible. Volcanoes serve the function of Mother Earth's lungs and like the body's lungs, they are essential for the movement and expression of the life force. Earth's very environment was made possible as a result of volcanic activity, which shaped the Earth's landscape with many of its mountains, islands, and plains. It is truly a stunning parallel in the way that earth's molten magma and its gases created life as it passed through Mother Earth's lungs (volcanoes). This is comparable to the rising Kundalini energy within the body as well as the breath that sustains human life as it passes through the body's lungs—both are endemic to life and are deeply interconnected. So imagine the power when you, geographically speaking, stand on an area over which there is seismic and geothermal activity— while placing your attention on the inner energy field of the body and the breath—a human volcanic eruption of Kundalini can become triggered.

Although not within the Pacific Ring of Fire, Iceland is among the world's most volcanically active places because it has thirty-five *active* volcanoes, and the geothermal activity there is remarkably intense. Despite Jeannette's cognitive and physical declines, Jeannette's daughter and I have planned a trip to Iceland next month as a special adventure in celebrating life and to take Jeannette to the warm geothermal pools there.

When the inner energy field of the body and the breath are recognized by the finder to be the powerhouse that they are, and effective spiritual practice is initiated with discipline, the Kundalini energies within us begin to ignite; however, this ignition is one of expanding *stillness*, not a literal heat. It is the physical body that may become hot, not the stillness itself. Although the body may be experienced as warmth when stillness expands or is uncovered, it is stillness nonetheless that is "fueling" the arising Kundalini energies. Finally, the body's inner fire is understood to be none other than *stillness*. This expanding stillness is made possible by focus upon the inner energy field of the body and the breath. When it commingles with the energies of the inner fire of planet Earth, you awaken. Together, those energies become one in union, and a new being arrives on the scene.

Indeed, humanity's strong, unconscious pull toward sexual expression is none other than the arising of inner pulsating energies that seek to align with Mother Earth's arising geothermal energies. In other words, most of humanity has confused the soul's goal to awaken spiritually with that of a lesser need: the seeking of sexual satisfaction. Unfortunately, many people then get "stuck" in their sexuality, desiring a sexual outlet that redirects the Kundalini energy and remaining unaware of its greater use in awakening; however, the goals of the soul will not remain thwarted forever. Eventually, events conspire to knock even the sex addict, along with everyone else, off of the sexual focus cycle.

When Kundalini energies are able to arise within the human body in harmony with the ever-arising geothermal energies bursting out of mother Earth, an "orgasmic" union becomes possible. A burst of awakening is then unavoidable.

For the newly minted hybrid, the physical body and mental orientation goes through some changes. Some of those changes may be intense, but only temporary, as the human mind adjusts to its status as a tool used by the greater good. There are actually physiological changes to the brain as the mind evolves when enlightenment occurs. Dietary habits often change, as does a shift in the hybrid's source of "entertainment." In my case, it was not that a desire for a specific kind of food occurred, but rather, there was a loss of the desire for food altogether.

As a coincidental transition for both Jeannette and me occurred simultaneously on the dietary front, I joined her, preferring predominantly liquid nourishment from strained, homemade vegetable broth, fruit juices, powdered vitamins, and powdered super foods. Of course regular food is still consumed, but not all the time.

The changes in the way that my mind functions now seem quite disorienting within a world that operates differently. A source of pride in the past was my superb organizational skills; now it is challenging to grasp a sense of how much time is passing within an everyday context. Punctuality used to be my strong suit, but now I can't seem to get aligned with the hands on a clock. Quite often it feels as though ten minutes has passed when in fact it was two hours. This exact dynamic occurs with respect to the days of the week. Each day feels similarly wonderful, perfect, and peaceful, with no need whatsoever to remember its name. Perhaps this is only temporary, but I cannot seem to keep track of the days of the week, no matter how often I reference a calendar;

however, this has not greatly affected my ability to hold a job and keep appointments, although there have been some snafus.

If your true essence is the same thing as the present moment, then an enlightened state makes this truth manifest in daily living. Because there is only this moment, it doesn't at all *feel* like different days are being lived consecutively. Rather than being just one more mental concept, this truth becomes the waking reference point for the hybrid. Days change for others, but it is always the now for me. Past and future events are somewhat difficult to imagine and whenever I attempt to focus on either, my reference point veers right back to right now. Finding my car in a parking lot sometimes eludes me, and wandering happily searching for it is an adventure of sorts.

Like Jeannette, seeking out otherwise normal activities such as watching television, shopping, and the need for travel (for the purpose of entertainment) has dissolved. Of course, the hybrid can still partake of all such activities, but they, like any activity, are not sought for satisfaction or distraction. Once "filled up" with essence, nothing further need be added for a sense of completion.

Once the hybrid's lifelong push toward the realization of enlightenment has been achieved, there is only one movement toward creative expression still possible: the desire to be of service to others. Even so, there is no compulsion to "help," but rather, it becomes a natural part of living. This does not mean that a hybrid cannot eat food with others, watch television, fly across country, or earn a living. It means that these activities are no longer sought as a way to become nourished, relaxed, fulfilled, or compensated. Simply by virtue of holding a station of peace within the hybrid's immediate environment, they become helpful, even useful. Any additional expression of service can be offered, but there is no sense that work is being performed since the previous distinction between "work" and "play" completely dissolves.

The hybrid readily aligns with the present moment and is dis-identified from mind activity which might otherwise censor "going with the flow" as its current ebbs and flows throughout daily life. As a mere twig on the river, life is simple and sweet. The shelves of groceries in the market, the road home, although previously seen and traveled many times before, are now brand new. A fresh reference point emerges as the present moment. This new orientation is the ultimate in experience and brings a stable peace. At the deepest level, this is who we are, which is why the need to do or add anything is so noticeably absent. Action can still happen in earnest in order to meet deadlines and goals, but it is sourced from stillness. The doing is enjoyed thoroughly, but the end goal is not cherished and focused upon to the degree that it once was. Just this moment, in its simple perfection, produces everything needed for whatever perfect future unfolds.

When you become aware that you are actually the present moment itself—rather than someone who is *experiencing* something within the present moment—awakening is becoming real for you. The present moment is perfectly alive, so simple, so vibrating with life; finally you know that it *is* life, and you are it.

Freedom from identification with mental activity is the ultimate achievement for any human being. No role, form, or attribute can possibly match enlightenment's ecstatic gains because all roles, forms, and attributes are, by their nature, so short-lived and fleeting.

For thousands of years, since early scribes began to articulate the teachings of saints, sages, shamans, and spiritual teachers of many religions, all ancient texts without exception point to this possible transformation. Although the actual meaning of this illusive spiritual goal has become obscured—in the same way that your true essence has become obscured—the culprit for both is the same: the egoic mind structure with its dark shadow, the pain body. Ancient spiritual texts, handed down from generation to generation, speak about a "redemption," a "new world," a "rebirth," and a "paradise" that can only be arrived at through the process of dis-identification with compulsive thinking. But through eons of mind-based scribes, ego-centered religious leaders, and the egoic tendency of the general population, Big Brother Mind has ensured its survival by obscuring the way *out* of suffering. Entrance to "heaven" does not happen at death. It is a state of being that ensures continuous peace and everlasting well-being and can be accessed right now. Only through the mind's demise as a tyrant—functioning compulsively and dysfunctionally—is true peace and happiness possible.

As you awaken through effective spiritual practice, at no time will your mind understand or comprehend the awakening process, for a very important reason:

*YOU are awakening, not your mind. YOU are being uncovered from under the mind's dominance over you. So don't expect mental thought to help you comprehend the spiritual practice which you are invoking to initiate this resurrection.*

Naturally, the egoic thought structure, like any other entity, wants to survive. But compulsive thought can only survive in all of us at the expense of the human species. Like a parasite imbedded in a dog, it will kill its host, and thereby kill its own possibility for long-term existence. If you doubt this, simply take a look at the declining state of humanity and planetary trends. When entire species of animals begin to go extinct, humans find themselves somewhere in the pecking order; however, an awakening species, from humanoid to hybrid, would mean the end of our current patterns of decline.

Like the parasite, the egoic thought structure has no innate wisdom. It cannot recognize that its own doom is ultimately ensured no matter which route is taken: it either causes a slow death to the host and untold emotional suffering and its concomitant dysfunctional societal tendencies, or it ensures its own death by its host awakening spiritually and becoming enlightened.

The former route is painful. The mental suffering that most humans tolerate as normal is extraordinary when compared to the equanimity of a hybrid who may be living within the very same community or household with virtually identical "problems" or the DPs in their midst. The latter route has challenges, but those challenges are easily navigated, once you fully comprehend the nature of the obstacle: the mind that resists your awakening with the cunning and force of a stealth submarine.

In the most surprising example of a true miracle, approximately sixty days after my awakening, Jeannette's pain body seemed to have mostly dissolved, with only minor flair-ups. Despite the fact that she could no longer speak or comprehend complex ideas, she could indeed understand simple concepts, much like a three-year-old child. She communicated through grunting and pointing, and still recognized and related to me, family, and friends. When asked, she could communicate preferences such as preferring to wear a pink sweater or black jacket. She still dressed herself somewhat, although there was quite a bit of confusion at bedtime. She would dress in her nightgown, then start over and get dressed in street clothes, putting on her shoes.

The precise mechanics of her own pain body's apparent dissolution may be, in part, attributed to her brain's inability to further utilize and thus dramatize her trapped essence. It's possible that, in her case, the pain body was simply no longer able to function as a pain body; however, this does not explain how so many other late-stage Alzheimer's patients continue *their* most aggressive behavior, right up to their death, demonstrating in full glory the "ugly" part of the disease.

As was mentioned previously, as the pain body dissolves, previously trapped consciousness is released, and *you* regain that lost essence. This is the source of the hybrid's newfound power station. This explains the sudden infusion of potent life force of any awakened person, and perhaps also explains why Jeannette uncharacteristically became as sweet and tender as a newborn kitten at this stage. Now, remarkably, wherever she goes and whomever she meets—the stranger in the pharmacy, a neighbor or friend, whether she knows them or not—Jeannette greets others as though she's beholding a long lost loved one and she showers them with emotional hugs and kisses. To those who know her, it's a miraculous development, as if she's been secluded on an island without outside communication for sixty years, and then suddenly she's rescued. Her emotional reactions at seeing *anyone* are joyous, intense, and celebratory. This, then, is her return to her essence, as the pain body's inner critic falls silent. Like enlightenment itself, what an extraordinary transformation!

Trapped energies are held by the pain body and can continue to "trap" additional energy when it is activated and begins to feed with its dysfunctional pain-body waltz. Conversely, when a pain body dissolves, that trapped energy is released and becomes available for use, but not just by the person whose pain body dissolved. Although more of my own essence became available for me, it also flowed into Jeannette for use by her.

Like a ripple effect, there is more available essence for all, which in turn helped dissolve hers, in addition to the constant love and care from her family and friends. This is how a domino effect can take place on a planetary scale. Awaken yourself, and then help to awaken those within your environment, by your example, and by "flowing" out peace as your recaptured essence becomes useable by everyone.

Whereas previously, because I became naturally and outwardly affectionate as the awakening process drew near, I would kiss Jeannette's hand; now she is kissing mine. Despite my affectionate nature, she normally responded with annoyance and irritation; now, she is taking me in her arms. It is mystifying to witness such heretofore uncharacteristic displays of affection and appreciation. The transition and dissolution of her pain body is so marked that it's like observing the slow melting of a jagged glacier as it trickles into a chasm. One week her pain body reacted, producing nail marks and blood on my hand; the next week she leaves soft kisses on my arm as she lovingly strokes my hair while we drive around town. Compared to her usual constant spikes between harsh irritation and only momentary acceptance, her profound transformation is eerily prophetic: If this is what happens to a hardened and aggressive human being when the pain body dissolves, then there is no doubt about humanity's ability to right every wrong, balance every injustice, and brook every divide.

Certainly, over the previous three years, Jeannette demonstrated kindness and good cheer, enthusiasm and tenderness; however, it was predictably short-lived and was immediately usurped by the pain body's return, as if to remind me that it hadn't gone far from its feeding ground.

Despite her declining brain function, if Jeannette's pain body can dissipate, then anybody's can. She embodied the perfect DP. Similar to the way all difficult people interact, the mechanics of her constant objections and habit of being offended was remarkable in its power to mirror the mind's patterns as expressed by all of us. So take heart. Once recognized for what it is, the pain body has no real power. Although it's cunning and persistent, it ultimately cannot outshine the beam of light breaking through from your own essence. Like the way that geothermal energies can actually pierce solid rock in creating volcanoes, the power of your essence will also ultimately shine through.

Once you begin effective spiritual practice as an antidote to the ego's penchant for hysteria, you no longer are tricked by its urge to disrupt. Instead, your normal daily existence most naturally heeds the Beatles most beloved lyric: you will simply and beautifully just "Let It Be." When the hybrids' numbers begin to increase, perhaps a tipping point will be reached at some juncture and humans will bloom, spiritually; and there is no telling what we as a group may accomplish. In the meantime, learn of the nutty egoic patterns that block the way to this flowering.

Those patterns become strikingly predictable, once you recognize their particular characteristics. For example, imagine if you were attempting to complete a graduate course in school while married to someone who sabotaged your every move to graduate. Suppose your spouse regularly threw your textbooks and half-finished term papers in the trash; suppose your partner turns back your clocks daily, so that you are constantly late for class; suppose that your mate speaks privately to your professors, telling them that you are a closet cheat. This is the challenging path of the finder who decides to awaken. Because the pain body takes note of your inroads to weaken it, it does strengthen its resolve; however, once you gain momentum with your spiritual practice—to continue with the analogy of the graduate student—by calmly locking your term paper and textbook in a safe, wearing a watch that you ensure is correct, and demonstrating to your professor that your work is your own, you are on your way to graduating and nothing and no one can stop you.

Instead of adopting worldly strategies as a solution, as was required by the thwarted graduate student, all that you need in order to awaken is a willingness to recognize the way and manner of the egoic mind and pain body and how they operate. First observe them as they become active in *others*; then observe them as they become active within *you*. Then use your new strategy to outsmart them.

During the month just after awakening, I had to learn to drive a car all over again. Although the mechanics of driving a car and the rules of the road were known to me, my mind simply worked differently and some adjustment was necessary. I ran a stop sign and a red traffic light, and reminiscent of Jeannette, I got lost several times in familiar territory; however, no damage was done. At the time of my awakening, I felt the most indescribable inner joy imaginable. Laughing out loud with hearty mirth had become routine. The apparent problems and so-called setbacks that others so commonly express are observed to be self-induced by negative, compulsive thoughts. The nightmare of human drama was readily seen to be completely unnecessary. Yet, a very real desire to help others was ever-present, to assist them in awakening from the nightmare that so readily blinds and binds them.

Of course, everyone develops spiritually along their own perfect timeline. Those who are spiritually ripe, and thus ready to expand their awareness, are naturally drawn to the subject of self-realization as they are set on their path more firmly. Those who have no interest whatsoever or who do not yet comprehend the relevance of awakening are free to endure as many rounds of suffering as they choose, until they have had enough. The process of awakening brings an end to chronic mental suffering. But the readiness to invite spiritual development occurs in its own perfect way and in its own perfect moment.

Be alert, then, for your window of opportunity in order to awaken from your slumber. This book serves as an alarm clock. It's not that you're running late, it's just time to wake up because you've been asleep long enough. The river of life will flow a strong current toward you, delivering the most extraordinarily ironic package imaginable: a special problem or difficult person providing every nuance necessary for your enlightenment.

Once awakened from the deep sleep of the ages, the finder becomes a hybrid. The hybrid allows the play of form to unfold as it is, recognizing how the simplicity of essence and the complexity of humanity will awkwardly dance into the night until a harmonious rhythm has naturally emerged.

This is the way out of suffering. This is the path to freedom. May you now be free.

A strong warm wind blows the cresting ocean waves as Jeannette and I drive along Pacific Coast Highway in Malibu. En route to her doctor's appointment, I watch her as she watches the ocean, a deep azure blue that stretches to meet the sky. How is it that they have suddenly become so similar, Jeannette and the sea?

Normally, the strong set of her jaw and her tightly crossed arms would have given away her displeasure, but not now. Today, there is no Alzheimer's; no moans of despair. Bedecked in two wristwatches, fingers full of rings, and holiday themed earrings in October, she then removes a plastic sheet of children's stickers from her purse and gingerly makes a selection by peeling it off the page. Triumphant, she holds it up for me to see, a small plastic "ruby" which she applies to the back of her hand, and then she adheres one to mine. Her joyful expression lights up the car, and we are frozen there in time as I look deeply in her eyes. Gone is her sadness, gone is the anger. Gone, gone, forever gone.

But wait, there *she* is—the invisible essence of her is beaming, so palpable—an exquisite alive peace. Unmistakably spilling out through her eyes, *she* is there in all her glorious, unchanging essence, the very same essence that makes up the primal forces of nature. As our eyes meet, mine are in tears, for the gift that she is.

*Peace will not come until we see the flaws in our own selves and struggle to efface them, until each of us realizes our individual uniqueness, and we each attune our very special selves to their perfection.*

*According to the Kabbalah, redemption is not an event that will take place all at once at the "end of days" nor is it something that concerns the Jewish people alone. It is a continual process, taking place at every moment.*

—Abraham Joshua Heschel, *Prayerbook for the Days of Awe*

# Acknowledgments

I AM DEEPLY GRATEFUL to Jeannette for opening her life to me and for allowing me to share this most profound journey with her. We have laughed and cried together over these past three years, and we have become very close and even affectionate. I extend my deepest appreciation to each and every member of Jeannette's immediate and extended family, for their love and constant emotional support. To Jeannette's grown kids and her sisters, whose friendship made all the difference in our day-to-day routine, and whose shared laughter brought out the best in all of us, it has been a joy to get to know each of them as we have traveled this road together.

To Jeannette's husband, whose most gracious gift of trust and consistent patience and his kind and gentle manner allowed my own process to reveal itself, I am grateful for his constant support and unstinting generosity in entrusting me with the care of his wife and encouraging me both as a caregiver and also as I wrote this manuscript. I am very thankful for his brilliant editorial comments and helpful feedback and for encouraging me with his early review of the manuscript.

I extend my gratitude to my publisher Robert S. Friedman, whose friendship and trust have made a huge impact on my life over the years. He has played a vital part in my ability to give creative expression to my innermost process, and for that I am eternally indebted to him.

I am thankful to John Nelson of Bookworks, editor extraordinaire, certainly one of the best editors on the planet. I am deeply grateful for his always creative and brilliant touch.

I am deeply thankful for my friends Xavier Jarquin and Alan Holt, whose friendship and love inspired me to clarify some of the processes in this book.

I am forever grateful to my father and my mother, Cecilia, for her love and friendship and for originally encouraging me to take the job as Jeannette's caregiver; to Harry and to my entire family—my sisters, brothers, and their wonderful spouses, and my nieces and nephews—whose love and laughter mean so much. I owe a special thank you to Mac, whose generosity and love came shining through; and to my son, Walter, whose compassion and zest for life lights up the world.

And finally, I am eternally grateful to Eckhart Tolle, without whom my spiritual deepening and this book may not have been possible.

# About the Author

Photo by Amy Williams

LISETTE LARKINS has had extraordinary paranormal experiences since childhood. Their import was to reveal to her the possibility of a "chronic state of well-being." She has published three books about these experiences, but it wasn't until she discovered the work of Eckhart Tolle on being "present" that a clear path presented itself. She began to apply these principles in her work as a publishing sales director, author, and spiritual guide. Stymied, she was guided in 2008 to take a job as Jeannette's caregiver, a patient with Alzheimer's disease, an experience that pushed her into a permanent state of "presence" and allowed her to formulate the principles expressed in *Difficult People.*

Lisette lives in Malibu, California, and can be reached at:

www.lisettelarkins.com
or on Facebook
or
Lisette Larkins
P.O. Box 481
Malibu, CA 90265

Rainbow Ridge Books publishes spiritual
and metaphysical titles and is distributed by Square
One Publishers in Garden City Park, New York.

To contact authors and editors, peruse our titles, and
see submission guidelines, please visit our website at:

www.rainbowridgebooks.com.

For orders and catalogs, please call toll-free:
(877) 900-BOOK